RICHARD M. NIXON

RICHARD M. NIXON

by Arthur J. Hughes

Illustrated with photographs

DODD, MEAD & COMPANY

NEW YORK

Copyright © 1972 by Arthur J. Hughes

ISBN: 0-396-06642-9
Library of Congress Catalog Card Number: 72-3152

Printed in the United States of America
by The Cornwall Press, Inc., Cornwall, N. Y.

To Charles McGoldrick

ACKNOWLEDGMENTS

◒◓◒

WHEN AN AUTHOR writes a book, he incurs many happy obligations. His determination taxes the patience, cooperation, and good humor of those closest to him to the fullest. Heartfelt thanks, therefore, go to Irene and the "Six J's" for putting up with this, the author's third published book.

The cooperation of friends, classmates, and associates of Richard Nixon was indispensable to this work. Thanks are expressed to Professor Paul Smith, Coach Wallace "Chief" Newman, Merle West, Lois Gaunt, Mrs. L. M. Dorn, Mrs. George Tani, Mrs. William Simmons, Clint Harris, Mel Rich, Harry Schuyler, Dr. C. Richard Arena, Edward Flutot, William Barton, Dean Roy Newsom, Judge Merton G. Wray, Richard Thomson, Edwin Wunder, and Kenneth Ball, as well as to the staffs of the libraries at Whittier College, the Town of Whittier, St. John's University, and, above all, to Brother Lawrence Drowne and Irving Wood of the McGarry Library of St. Francis College.

The St. Francis College Research Committee, which generously aided in the form of travel and other funds, is most gratefully acknowledged.

The master craftsmen of the publishing business, the editors, must also be acknowledged, since they take an uneven, unpolished hulk and hone it into a smooth and streamlined vessel for the author's ideas. Where this book sails along nicely, the credit should go to Dorothy Bryan and Rosemary Casey of Dodd, Mead & Company. The author takes the responsibility for the rough seas. Thanks are also due to Professor Michael Casey of St. Francis College and Brigid Casey for cheerfully maintaining close lines of communication between writer and editor; to Helen Winfield of Dodd, Mead's Production Department, and to William W. Parish of the White House Photo Office.

Finally, the author wishes to express special thanks to a wise and valued friend whose interest in the Hughes family led to the dedication of this book to him—Charles McGoldrick.

RICHARD M. NIXON

CHAPTER I

ᘓᔓᘏ

ON JULY 4, 1971, President Richard Milhous Nixon met with dozens of lawmakers, judges, and other officials at the National Archives in Washington, D.C., where an original copy of the Declaration of Independence is kept. The President, Chief Justice Warren Burger, and Speaker of the House Carl Albert then spoke to the people of America and the world over television and radio. The purpose of this gathering, the President explained, was to open the Bicentennial Era, that five-year period planned to usher in the two hundredth anniversary of the birth of the United States. He expressed the earnest wish that the United States would lead all nations toward a period of permanent peace. And more, he hoped that this peaceful world would be an open one, with "open borders, open hearts, open minds."

Nearly two centuries earlier, another Nixon had been associated with a patriotic message, this time the Declaration of Independence, which was read for the first time in public at Philadelphia on July 8, 1776. This was George, a newly married man who, at the age of twenty-four, left his farm and his bride to join a fighting outfit from Delaware. He enlisted as a private and rose to the rank of ensign during the Revolutionary War. He was present with the Continental Army during General Washington's campaign of 1776, crossing the Delaware River in December. Several weeks later, following the surprise attack upon the Hessians at Trenton, New Jersey, George Nixon took part in an engagement against the British, outside Princeton. He was in the thick of the conflict, wielding his sword and battle pike vigorously in his new nation's struggle.

Their victories of December, 1776, and January, 1777, gave the sagging morale of the Patriots a great boost. And it spurred Washington's soldiers on to face fresh sacrifices and dangers. George Nixon served as a spy and a scout for the rebels against the Redcoats during this period.

The war over, he returned to his home in Delaware. Like many Americans, however, he heard the call of the frontier and sold his Delaware farm. Packing up their belongings, the Nixon family moved to Pennsylvania, where George bought a 224-acre farm for sixteen hundred dollars. It was located in a "pleasant little valley" near Washington, Pennsylvania, a small town of some eight hundred inhabitants. Many years later, when he was in his seventies, George moved farther westward with part of his family, this time to Ohio. Some years after that, when he was about ninety years old, George moved once again, to Illinois. This state became his last resting place. The sword he carried and the uniform he wore during the Revolutionary War went with him as he pioneered across the country.

George Nixon's strong example of devotion to a noble cause was passed on to his descendants. One of his grandsons, George Nixon III, who lived in Ohio, answered the call for Union Army volunteers during the War Between the States. George was a farmer, as were most of the northern fighting men at that time, but in other ways he was not a typical Union soldier. For one thing, he was forty years old, and for another, he was the father of nine children.

On July 1, 1863, George's outfit, the 73rd Regiment from Ohio, moved up to the front lines at Gettysburg, Pennsylvania, to take part in what became one of the greatest battles in the war. For two days, the Ohioans suffered casualties from sniper and artillery fire. On the third day, George fell, severely wounded. One account of what followed stated that George lay for hours between the Union and Confederate lines, until he was rescued by a teen-age comrade who crawled into "no man's land" and dragged him back to the Union side.

For the next few days, George Nixon fought gallantly to hold onto his life, but, at length, he lost his final battle. He now lies buried among the heroes of Gettysburg, one of the last to die there. Less than two years later, George Nixon's children were left orphans when his wife Margaret died. George and Margaret were Richard Nixon's great-grandparents. One of their sons, Samuel Brady Nixon, was the President's grandfather.

Thus George Nixon's service to the cause of Independence in July, 1776, his grandson's sacrifice of his life in July, 1863, and Richard Nixon's opening of the Bicentennial Era with a call for "the building of an open world," link the Nixon family closely to the American Republic.

*   *   *

Like his ancestors, Richard Milhous Nixon, thirty-seventh President of the United States, has lived closely with many important events of American history. From the time he served as a young naval officer in the war against Japan in the Pacific, on through the days of his Presidency, he has played an active part, sometimes small, sometimes great, in the development of his country.

The two families from which the President descended, the Nixon and Milhous families, have long associations with the country. The incomplete records of colonial times date the arrival of the first Milhouses at 1729. In that year, two Quaker emigrants named Thomas and Sarah Milhous left the village of Timahoe, in County Kildare, Ireland, and journeyed to the New World. A few years later, the first Nixon arrived, also from Ireland.

Neither family knew the other, but they had a good deal in common. They were farmers who loved the land and sacrificed greatly in order to purchase holdings on which to raise their crops and their children. Not all members of the family wanted to stay on the Atlantic coast, however, and as time passed, some Nixons and Milhouses made their way west. At one time, Nixons and Milhouses lived only nine miles apart, yet did not meet. It was not until the families branched out to California that they were united in the persons of two young immigrants to that state—Indiana-born Hannah Milhous and Francis (Frank) Nixon from Ohio, the parents of Richard Nixon.

Hannah and Frank met because of two unrelated facts. First, Hannah, like her ancestors, was a member of the Society of Friends, sometimes called Quakers, a tolerant, peace-loving, hard-working, Bible-reading religious group. Secondly, Frank Nixon nearly froze his feet off while driving a trolley car in the bitter cold weather of Ohio.

Closely knit members of the Society of Friends had communities located throughout the entire United States during the nineteenth century. For many years, they had been a persecuted sect, staunchly standing up for the principles of religious liberty, racial tolerance, and peace among nations. They were not showy people; they did not believe in demonstrating their beliefs with outward displays of emotion, elaborate rituals, or hymn-singing. This type of religious experience was right for many people but it did not satisfy most Friends. They did not have ordained clergymen, preferring at their meetings to share periods of quiet meditation with each other, broken only when members of the group were moved to speak. They hoped to be guided in life's decisions by an "Inner Light" given them by the Holy Spirit.

By the end of the nineteenth century, organized persecution of the Friends had died out, but they still tended to stick closely together so they could help each other and preserve their faith. One reason for this closeness was their size. In 1913, the year that Richard Nixon was born, there were only 125,000 Quakers in the entire United States. With such a comparatively small number, word of their doings traveled quickly among them. That is why, when a group of Friends decided to build a settlement in Southern California, the family of Hannah Milhous heard of it in Indiana.

The new California town was named Whittier, after the

New England "Quaker poet," John Greenleaf Whittier, who was so proud of the honor the founders paid him that he dedicated a poem to their new venture. Today, Whittier is a bustling city of over 72,000 people, with eleven banks, over seventy houses of worship, and many important modern industries, such as factories for making aircraft and missile parts. But in the 1880's, when it was first settled, it was a quiet farm area, fifteen miles east of Los Angeles. A sprawling ranch of over twelve hundred acres, owned by an Indiana farmer named John Thomas, was sold to a land company owned by Quakers Aquilla and Hannah Pickering, Jonathan and Rebecca Bailey, and others.

The first business in Whittier was the real estate business, as the company began to sell off land in home sites and farm acreage. The railroads helped the town to grow by selling one-way tickets to the settlers at low rates. Soon Quakers from all over the country were laying out a thousand dollars for a five-acre farm or between one and two hundred dollars for a town site. Houses began to dot the area.

With their zeal for hard work and their willingness to cooperate with each other, the newcomers turned their lands into profitable enterprises. Apricots, oranges, lemons, walnuts, pumpkins, and cabbages could be grown in this area, but later these crops had to compete with oil derricks when "black gold" was discovered in Whittier. As word spread that the new town was a good place in which to make a living and raise a family, people poured into the community.

In 1897, ten years after the founding of Whittier, Hannah's parents, Franklin and Almira Milhous, packed up their nine children and their household goods and left Indiana. Franklin, who was a nurseryman, brought along his farm livestock and even his trees on the long rail trip. Hannah was twelve years old at the time.

Arriving in Southern California, the senior Milhouses bought several acres of good farm land, put in their trees, built a fine sturdy house, and promptly sent the children off to school. All members of their sect felt that education was a good means of becoming a better person, a better Friend, and a better American. Even today, over the entrance to one of their schools, there is the inscription: "What you would have in the life of a nation you must first put into its schools," carved by Whittier citizens.

The Friends tried to instill in their children a love of mankind which would make them truly tolerant of all races and religions. Just as earlier Milhouses had helped runaway slaves seek freedom on the "Underground Railway" in the Midwest before the War Between the States, so Almira Milhous, Hannah's mother, invited Mexican, Indian, and any other persons who worked for them or were their friends to share their table as equals, no matter what their race or religion might be.

The Milhous family flourished and became highly respected in Whittier, and it is possible to trace much of this prosperity back to the fact that they lived their faith.

Now for the second fact behind the meeting of Hannah Milhous and Frank Nixon—the latter's frozen feet. Frank Nixon was born and raised on an Ohio farm, the grandson of the George Nixon III who had lost his life at Gettysburg. Frank had a hard life as a boy. His mother died after a long illness when he was only seven. Frank and his brothers and sisters were required to put in hours of farm chores every day and, in addition, the boys helped their father haul heavy logs to a lumber mill to increase the family income. They did not have much chance for schooling. Frank quit after the fourth grade. Their father had been a schoolteacher, however, and knew how to give his children basic instruction in reading and arithmetic.

Frank was not naturally a stay-at-home so he hired himself out as a farmhand in the 1880's. At the rate of twenty-five cents a day and his "keep" he might never become a millionaire, but life did have some advantages. He had a fine sorrel which he proudly rode all over the county. Everyone recognized his handsome mount and Frank took the opportunity to show it off any time he could. Even though his family belonged to the Democratic party, Frank could not resist the chance to join a parade in honor of William McKinley, who was a Republican candidate for office, in the early 1890's. Young Frank decked out his fine steed so successfully that the Republicans put both horse and rider close to Mr. McKinley in the line of march.

William McKinley had grown up on an Ohio farm himself and he knew horses well. He praised the sorrel highly, and Frank glowed with pride and never forgot the incident. Later in his life, he related that Mr. McKinley had asked him how he was going to vote, even though the boy was then only in his teen years. Frank shot back, "Republican," and it was Mr. McKinley's turn to smile with pleasure. When he was eligible, Frank Nixon joined the Republican party and he remained loyal to it all his life, raising his family in its beliefs.

Like many young men of his day, Frank was a restless fellow, always wondering what was on the other side of the hill. And, since he had been raised on a farm, he could do almost any job well enough to earn a living at it. He was handy with tools and, at one time or another, was employed as a carpenter, house painter, telephone lineman, potato farmer, oil field worker, Pullman-car painter, and sheep rancher. For a year and a half he lived in Colorado, spending part of his time installing telephones throughout the state.

After his stay in Colorado, Frank returned to Ohio and became a streetcar motorman in Columbus. This was a tough and uncomfortable job, and it was made even more difficult because the operator had to stand in an open vestibule at the front of the car with no protection from wind, rain, or snow. During one winter, Frank suffered frostbite while driving in the unheated, drafty vestibule, and he soon began to long for a warm climate to bring the life back into his chilled toes. Before he left the job, though, he organized his fellow conductors and led a successful fight to have a law passed which required the trolley-car owners to install closed vestibules.

In 1907, Frank said good-bye to the bitter winters in Columbus and started off for Southern California. Unlike Franklin and Almira Milhous, who moved to their "Promised Land" with so many of their Indiana belongings, Frank Nixon brought himself and his hopes and very little else. He was the kind of American whom a later President, Herbert Hoover, would call a "rugged individualist." He was proud to stand on his own two feet, never refused any kind of work as long as it was honest, and never patted himself on the back for doing his duty.

He first took a job with the Pacific Electric Railway Company as a trolley-car motorman. For eighteen cents an hour, he piloted his rattling red trolley between Los Angeles and Whittier, which was still a rural area, far from the busy city streets of "L.A." Something about the placid town attracted Frank. Maybe it was the neat houses, the trim fields, or the sense of joy in work he shared with the residents. Or maybe it was the prim and proud girls with their starched dresses and broad-brimmed hats. He settled down in Whittier, and it did not matter that he was a Methodist and not a Quaker, he was accepted all the same.

After a while, Frank gave up his motorman's job and became a hired hand on a farm near Whittier. Early in 1908, he met Hannah Milhous at a church social. A few months later, the two were married. The first child born to them was a son whom they named Harold. The young family moved several times in the first few years, perhaps because Frank still had a bit of the wanderlust in him.

This all changed when Frank and Hannah hit upon the idea of taking up lemon growing. They moved to the town of Yorba Linda, a sandy stretch of California about twenty miles south of Whittier. They bought a ten-acre site near the center of town and planted a lemon grove. With his own hands, Frank built a snug, one-and-a-half story bungalow for his wife and son. And outside their front bedroom window they planted a pepper tree.

Then the hard work began. It takes years for a new grove

to bear fruit, so Frank turned to his other talents to support his family. These included carpentry. He helped his neighbors construct warehouses and homes, some of which are still standing today. In between these chores, he irrigated his grove, cultivating and fertilizing it lovingly. Of course, there was always the family livestock to care for, as well as the garden.

The Nixons' second son, Richard Milhous Nixon, was born in Yorba Linda on January 9, 1913, in the front bedroom of their home. Hannah picked the name because of her admiration for King Richard, known as Lion-heart, of England. Three more sons were to join the family later—Donald, Arthur, and Edward.

For the first nine years of his life, Richard Nixon lived in Yorba Linda. These were not easy times for the family, since the lemon grove was not profitable. Although the region was good for this fruit in general, the trees did not thrive on the particular site owned by the Nixons. The soil there was not the most suitable, and weather conditions hampered growth, too.

There were times when money was scarce and all the family had to eat was corn meal, but usually there was enough plain food to satisfy everyone. An ingenious housewife could turn salt pork, round steak, beans, onions, tomatoes, and potatoes into a family feast. And if the genius happened to be Hannah Nixon, the repast could be topped off with one of her famous pies, particularly cherry, which became Richard's favorite. After dinner, Hannah would settle down to making and mending clothes for her growing family.

For a boy, there was always something to do in Yorba
Linda, and someone with whom to do it. If Dick's older
brother, Harold, was busy, he could always play with Donald, who was a year and a half younger than he. Or they
could play with their cousin Merle West, who lived about
two hundred feet away from them, across the Anaheim irrigation ditch. This was a trench about ten or twelve feet
wide and a few feet deep which the local water company
used to supply the entire region. Although it was a shallow
watercourse, it had steep sides with the stream flowing
swiftly through them. It was particularly attractive to the
Nixon boys, since it ran right outside their front door, no
more than thirty feet from their house. On summer days,
all the neighborhood boys would jump into the ditch and
swim and splash the dust off, sometimes while still wearing
their overalls.

Swimming was strictly forbidden, not only because a
small boy could be drowned in the swift current but also
because people down the line drank the water. This meant
that the boys had to watch out for ditch-riders, tough in-
spectors from the water company who patrolled the banks
to keep the stream clear of debris and small boys. One ditch-
rider had threatened to cut off the boys' ears and make a
sandwich out of them if he caught them in the ditch. This
made them particularly cautious and ready to scramble up
the bank when they were alerted. Another danger to watch
out for was Frank Nixon, who would give it to his boys if
he caught them in the swift waters.

At other times, the boys explored the rolling countryside,
playing among the trees of the orchards and up and down

the gullies, racing barefoot or riding scooters along the dusty roads, practicing with their slingshots, chasing after rabbits, or fishing in the nearby lake. On weekends, sometimes, there was picnicking in the mountains, reached by the family buckboard. It was hard to escape nature in the town of Yorba Linda; it was everywhere—in the sun, in the sandy soil, and in the smooth slopes to the east.

Life in Yorba Linda offered some real adventures for Dick and Harold Nixon. One of these was visiting the local blacksmith, peering into the mysterious darkness of his shop, lighted by the fire at the forge, and watching the sparks fly wildly as the smith's hammer struck hard on the hot metal of a horseshoe. The two boys never tired of the scene. Another favorite adventure for the pair was to help an older friend named John deliver groceries to nearby farmers. Not only was it fun riding over the back roads to the various farmhouses but at the end, there would be a few pennies for each boy for his service.

One adventure Dick had was not a pleasant one. It happened when he was so young, only three years old, he barely remembered it. He was driving in the family buggy with his mother, his little brother Donald, and a neighbor girl, who was supposed to be holding him safe. As the buggy turned a curve near the irrigation ditch, Dick tumbled over the side. One of the wagon wheels cut a deep slash in his scalp. Knowing that only at a hospital could such a wound be treated properly, his mother was desperate, since the nearest hospital was miles away. She thought quickly, then rushed to the home of the only neighbor in town who owned an automobile. After a wild ride, the boy was given emergency treatment and the gash was sewn up. Although it is covered by his hair, Richard Nixon still carries that long scar today.

One of the happy experiences Dick Nixon had in Yorba Linda came in 1918, when he was five years old. His grandmother, Almira Milhous, came to take care of him and his two brothers, Harold, nine, and Don, aged three, while their mother went to the hospital to have her fourth baby. After three boys, Frank and Hannah were sure this would be a girl, but they were wrong and number four was named Arthur. The boys went to the hospital to see the newcomer and thereafter the baby had three loyal protectors to look after him.

When Dick Nixon dreamed of his future, as all young people do, his imagination turned to the most adventurous job he knew of—railroading. At night, in his room at the back of the house, he would listen to the trains of the Pacific Electric passing nearby. Then he would think of all the places to which he would travel when he grew up and became a locomotive engineer. Another reason why he chose this field was that one of the Nixons' neighbors, who was a railroad engineer, seemed to make a good living at it.

Richard Nixon never did get to work on a railroad, but he did satisfy his desire to go places and see things, even surpassing his father as a traveler. On one journey as Vice President, he logged over 45,000 miles. Most of his trips have been by air, though, something he might not have dreamed much about as a boy, since flying was then very experimental.

The young Nixons, like boys everywhere, were happiest

when they were on the move. It could be running, riding one of the farm horses, speeding along on an old scooter, or curling up in a worn-out tire and rolling down a hill. At first, the family owned a buckboard to which the farm horses were harnessed for long trips. In 1919, however, when Dick was five, Frank and Hannah Nixon acquired their first car, an Overland. The boys were always eager to pile into it and go anywhere they could. Like all early autos, the Nixons' vehicle was not too reliable, particularly for a long trip. But this did not stop Frank, the incorrigible traveler, from packing everyone aboard and driving to San Francisco or even to Yosemite for an outing. His wife was not so adventurous on her own, but she would drive the car across town to visit her friend Mrs. Barton and find out how her son Bill was doing in the Navy during World War I. Dick probably didn't realize it, because he was very young, but Yorba Linda was a lonely place during the war years (1917–1918) when some twenty-three local boys joined the armed forces, to "Answer Mr. Wilson's Call," as the popular song went.

Much later, Woodrow Wilson, who was elected President two months before Dick was born, would influence the latter's life greatly. In 1916, when President Wilson ran for a second term, Hannah Nixon was so inspired by his speeches and writings on peace that she voted for him, even though he was a Democrat and the Nixons were still Republicans. The split vote in the Nixon home—Hannah for Democrat Wilson and Frank for the Republican candidate, Charles Evans Hughes—was a topic for discussion for years afterward. When Richard Nixon became President in 1969, he said that Woodrow Wilson had inspired his mother "with his idealism and she in turn passed that on to me."

So Dick Nixon became interested in politics early in his life, a lot earlier than most young Americans. And since he saw his father reading the newspaper to get the facts (this was before radio and TV), it was natural for Richard to do the same. Even before he knew how to read, he could be found lying on the floor pretending to absorb the items in the local paper. His mother was pleased with this interest and began teaching him to read before he went to school. Other mothers in that day started the education of their children early, too, so when it came time for them to go to school, many of the first-graders were far advanced. Hannah Nixon believed it was very important for every person to get every scrap of education he could as early as he could. By the time her son marched off barefoot to the little red building across town which served as the school, he knew how to read. He burned with a desire to learn, partly because of the example his mother and father showed him, which started the fire, but mostly because of his own interest, which served as the sustaining fuel.

There was not enough space in the Yorba Linda school to allow each class to have its own room. Two consecutive grades therefore shared the same classroom. Dick always managed to sit near the pupils in the higher class and, since he already knew the work of his own grade, he began to soak up the studies of the next year. He did this so well that he was able to skip the third grade. He was a "bright, well-behaved boy," according to one of his teachers, and very quiet. Because of his reading ability, he won as an award a copy of *Black Beauty*, which he prized for years.

Although he knew how to have fun and enjoy life as much as any of the other children, he was basically a serious boy, not the kind who fools around in school and gets into trouble with his teachers. He made it a habit to be on time for class, was rarely absent, and always earned good grades.

His mother and father knew they had a promising family for which they were grateful. To help their children take advantage of their talents, they provided them with outside interests. Because they thought Dick might have musical ability, they acquired a big upright mahogany piano and started him taking lessons on it when he was seven. He was also given violin lessons at this time.

Dick Nixon learned how to play the piano moderately well and was even invited to play for religious service. Some Friends in the community frowned on music in the meeting-house, but others were coming around to the idea that a hymn or two was good for the soul and gave a lift to the careworn and hard-working members.

The Nixons were devout people who assembled every morning to read a passage from the Bible. Each took a turn at reading, so that the children not only had a religious exercise but also gave Frank and Hannah some idea of their progress in school. Four times a week, once on Wednesday and three times on Sunday, the Nixons and their fellow Quakers went to the little Friends' meetinghouse, just down the street from the school. Sunday School was one of the most important parts of the children's week and the Nixon boys were very proud of their father, who taught there after he converted from the Methodist to the Quaker faith.

Frank and Hannah Nixon took life seriously and they taught their children to do the same. To them, work was not just something you did to earn enough money to support yourself and have a little left over for enjoyment. Work was life and life was work—this was what God had planned for man. Without hard work, the Nixons would not have known what to do with themselves.

This does not mean that they were gloomy in their outlook on life or always occupied in grinding labor. They took pleasure in their work and also in their family outings and in their gatherings with friends and neighbors. They enjoyed worshipping God. They loved music, and they gloried in the warmth of the climate and the fertile land of California. But mostly, they knew the deep satisfaction of a job well done.

Years later, as President, Richard Milhous Nixon remembered the standards taught and demonstrated to him by his parents and tried to pass on to the people of the United States how he felt about them. He was addressing his countrymen on Labor Day, so it was appropriate that he should speak of work. He called his concept the "competitive spirit" or the "work ethic." The terms used were not important, but the ideals behind them revealed the character of Richard Nixon better, perhaps, than any other public speech.

The President said: "The competitive spirit goes by many names. Most simply and directly, it is called the *work ethic*. As the name implies, the work ethic holds that labor is good in itself, that a man or woman at work not only makes a contribution to his fellow man but becomes a better person by virtue of the act of working.

"That work ethic is ingrained in the American character. That is why most of us consider it immoral to be lazy or slothful, even if a person is well enough off not to have to work. . . ."

A few days after he delivered this speech to the American people, President Nixon repeated the message to the Congress. "Hard work is what made America great," he said, and added that no work is "beneath a person's dignity if it provides food for his table and clothes and shelter for his children." Only work can give a person the good life, he declared, and the good life is not just having a lot of fun. "The good life is the active, productive, working life—the life that gives as well as gets."

This is the basic philosophy of Richard Milhous Nixon. He learned it by seeing his parents live it. He learned it by doing the chores he was given to do—in the kitchen, in the orchard, in the barn. And, of course, this home training was reinforced both at school and at the meetinghouse.

CHAPTER II

❧

WHEN RICHARD NIXON was nine years old, he and his family moved to Whittier. The year was 1922. It had not been an easy decision for his parents to make, but, after much discussion, they had agreed to give up their Yorba Linda farm. In addition to the fact that their lemon trees had never flourished because of the combination of poor soil and bad weather, was the poor market price for lemon crops, which hit the Nixons at the time of their first harvest. Then, Hannah Nixon had always lived in fear of her children drowning in the Anaheim Ditch. No matter how much they threatened and punished their boys, the presence of an inviting stream so close to their house was too tempting. And, perhaps Frank Nixon felt that it was time to move on. After all, they had first settled in Yorba Linda in 1912. They had been there ten years. That was long enough.

The Nixon move was not a stampede. Frank Nixon subdivided his acres and sold the land off piece by piece, a great part of it going to the school system, which now owns most of this property.

From one of the oldest of man's occupations, fruit raising, the Nixons turned to what was then the newest—the gasoline business. Not many people then were as farsighted and venturesome, because the automobile, like the computer in our own day, sort of "crept up" on America. In 1900, less than 4200 passenger cars, worth under five million dollars, were sold in the United States. In the year 1920, almost two million cars were sold for over $1,800,000,000. Auto travel became very popular. Americans logged nearly sixty-eight million miles in 1922 and used over five billion gallons of gasoline. Highways were being built at a rapid rate, thanks to a federal highway program of aid to states. The dirt roads of America, which turned into rushing streams or muddy scars on the landscape whenever bad weather struck, were being transformed gradually into all-weather paved highways.

Since there was no gas station between Whittier and La Habra, a small town about eight miles to the southeast, Frank Nixon purchased an acre of land and opened one. It was located on East Whittier Boulevard, which was a main road consisting only of two dirt lanes. This old highway, dating back to the Mexican period in California history, runs northwest from Whittier into the heart of downtown Los Angeles.

Business was so good that sometimes the cars actually lined up to buy fuel. Frank Nixon's gamble in an unknown field paid off. However, in this decision, he had not really been so lucky, at least according to a family story. His wife had wanted him to buy a different parcel of land for the service station. He hadn't agreed and, as a result, lost out financially, for the site of her choice proved to be rich in oil.

It became a family joke—how close to great wealth they had been.

The service station drew in a comfortable living for the family, since the Nixon location was a good one in spite of its lack of oil wells. Back of the station was the Nixon house. It was a simple home, but it was spacious enough for the parents and their four sons.

For the convenience of his customers, Frank Nixon began selling milk and bread as well as gas and oil. This sideline became so profitable that he decided to expand on it, and, when the meetinghouse where the Friends worshipped was replaced by a newer structure, Mr. Nixon bought the old building and moved it to his land, turning it into "Nixon's Market."

The Nixons began to stock everything that the neighboring farmers needed—meat, vegetables, canned goods, kerosene, fruit, and animal fodder. A steadily increasing number of people came to buy there, sometimes from miles away. They found that Frank Nixon was a fair man, not out to make a fortune from his customers, many of whom were friends or relatives of the family. Also, he and his wife permitted charge accounts, which helped the cash-poor shoppers of the neighborhood. And the many Mexicans and Japanese who lived and worked in the region also received a welcome at the store.

The Nixon boys found life a lot faster-moving in Whittier than it had been in Yorba Linda. There were more people around, more friends to play with, a bigger school to attend. Harold and Richard took turns pumping gas and checking oil, enjoying the sense of importance it gave them.

One of the joys of the Nixon household was Arthur, the pet of the family, since he was the youngest at this time. He brought a smile to everyone's face, especially when he did something a little devilish. Once, at the age of five, Arthur took some cigarettes from the store and began smoking them in the back yard. A neighbor told on him, but it didn't go too hard with him, for the Nixons rarely chastised their children severely. Their mother never struck them and their father reserved his strong arm for only the gravest "crimes."

Between working in the gas station and the store, there was not very much time just for fun, but once in a while the boys were able to go to a movie or to the beach. Even though the family had enough for essentials, there was never much extra money in the Nixon home and the boys did not receive allowances. If they needed something special, they worked for it, picking fruit and vegetables for nearby farmers or doing other odd jobs. One of the toughest tasks Dick ever had was picking beans for one dollar a day.

Of all the advantages that living in Whittier gave the Nixon boys, they thought the greatest was in being near Grandmother Almira Milhous. She was one of those older relatives a young person never forgets—a friend who really listens to and cares about a boy, even one who is only a few feet tall. She made Dick and all the other young relatives realize that they were important, worthwhile persons. On their birthdays, she composed special poems just for them and made copies to present along with her other gifts.

On one of his birthdays, Dick received five dollars and a picture of Abraham Lincoln. Dick hung the portrait over his bed and it stayed there all through his years of growing up. On the picture, Grandmother Milhous had written out part of a poem by Longfellow:

> Lives of great men oft remind us
> We can make our lives sublime
> And departing, leave behind us
> Footprints on the sands of time.

Almira Milhous had taught her children to care about others, even as she did. So Richard's Aunt Edith Timberlake, his mother's sister, remembered her nephews' birthdays while raising her own family. She gave Dick a history of the United States on one of his birthdays, and he read it avidly.

As a result of this attention from their whole family—grandparents, aunts, uncles, and, of course, their own parents—Dick and his brothers were made to feel as if they were part of a united team. There were squabbles, naturally, but underneath it all was a kind of unity produced by the doctrine of tolerance that was a vital part of the faith of the Friends. At the Milhous table, the boys met people from all over and from all races, religions, and classes. Farm workers and other employees sat down to eat with the family and the conversation was apt to range over many interesting topics.

The variety of things in which his relatives were interested and the broad range of the conversations he heard in his own home and the homes of his relatives had an enduring effect on Dick. When his father spoke of current politics, the boy listened intently, and learned. Frank Nixon was pleased when the Republicans regained control of the federal government after 1920 but was shaken and disgusted by the scandals which were disclosed in 1924. The most famous of these was called the "Teapot Dome" Scandal (after an oil-rich place by that name in Wyoming), and it involved some high-ranking Republicans who were eventually fined and jailed for their crimes. Young Dick was saddened, too, by these revelations. In fact, it is possible that these stories changed his whole life because it was at this time that eleven-year-old Richard Nixon gave up the idea of becoming a railroad engineer. He told his mother that he was going to be a lawyer instead—"a lawyer who can't be bought," as he put it.

The leaders of America were personal, flesh-and-blood people to Dick Nixon and his family. And they were moral leaders as well as political figures. From his grandmother, Dick had learned to revere Abraham Lincoln, whom she considered one of the world's greatest men. From his mother, he received an image of the peace-making, world-viewing side of Woodrow Wilson. From his father, he learned to love the Republican party, its humanitarian principles, and its reform-minded leaders. Teddy Roosevelt was one of Frank Nixon's idols, and Dick, who was only six when the great TR died, imitated this veneration. In 1968, when running for President, Richard Nixon often mentioned how TR had thought that the Presidency should be a "bully pulpit," that is, that the President should be a moral leader as well as chief executive.

From 1922 until 1926, Dick attended East Whittier Elementary School, which was located in a beautiful Spanish-style building with soaring towers from which American flags were flown. The school, located down the boulevard from the Nixon Market, was attended by the three older Nixon boys, Dick starting in the fifth grade.

Once in school there, Dick Nixon soon found himself involved in what would become one of his most enjoyable activities—debating and public speaking. These are not the most popular of activities among young people. To some, even the thought of getting up in front of an audience is terrifying. To others, public debate is just as terrifying, but they overcome their fear because debate can be so exhilarating and also worthwhile in preparing for a future career. Dick Nixon belonged to the second group. One afternoon he came home from school and told his father that he had been assigned to debate another student on the subject of whether it was cheaper to rent or buy a home. Mr. Nixon, knowing the importance of being well prepared, helped his son to gather facts and figures. Dick proved his point, that renting was cheaper, and so won his first venture into public argumentation. From then on, debating played an increasingly large part in his life.

At school, Dick Nixon was as hard-working at his studies as he had been at Yorba Linda. At recess time, however, he joined in playing soccer and other games with his classmates.

When Dick was in the seventh grade, one of his teachers was Lewis Cox, a man who influenced him greatly. Mr. Cox taught physical education and impressed his students with the need to hang on and fight hard in everything they did. This, of course, backed up what Dick was being taught at home. He showed this tenacious trait when he was picked for debate on whether insects were more harmful than beneficial. He defended the insects, spending long hours in preparation and leaving no available angle of research unexplored in his effort to be thorough. He even enlisted the aid of one of his father's brothers, Ernest Nixon, a horticulturist.

To Hannah and Frank Nixon, as well as to their many relatives in California, young Richard was marked for great things. His grandmother thought he might become a preacher, perhaps because he spoke so well. His mother, however, felt that music might be the career for which he was destined. By the time he was twelve, he had been training for five years on the piano and the violin, under the expert eyes of Griffith Milhous, Hannah's brother. To advance him further, the Nixons sent Richard away to study with Hannah's sister, Jane Beeson, who was also a music teacher. Aunt Jane lived with her husband and children in Lindsay, California, several hundred miles away. Dick did not like being separated from his own family and looked forward eagerly to letters from home. He especially missed little Arthur, who had started the first grade that year.

When, at the end of the school session, his parents came for him, Dick was overjoyed. But his happiness was shadowed during that summer by the illness of Arthur. When the little boy was examined, the doctors could not diagnose the reason for his illness. All he wanted to do was sleep. Two weeks later, Arthur was dead. His parents and brothers were stunned. It was a blow they never forgot, even though they accepted it as a part of the Divine Plan.

Meanwhile, on a farm near the town of Artesia, California, less than ten miles from Whittier, a girl named

Thelma Catherine Patricia Ryan was growing up. She had been born in Ely, Nevada, where her father had worked as a miner before becoming a farmer in California. Since he was of Irish ancestry and his daughter had been born on March 16, the eve of St. Patrick's Day, he always called her "Pat."

The life of the Ryan family was hard and unrewarding. Their small pleasures were far outweighed by unending labor. When Pat Ryan was twelve, her mother died from cancer. So while Dick Nixon carried his grief for the loss of his brother Arthur, the farm girl whom he would later meet and marry was trying to become reconciled to the absence of her mother.

His year in the eighth grade became a memorable one for Richard Nixon, filled as it was with a sense of accomplishment and the knowledge that he would soon be a high-school student, well on the way to his goal of becoming a lawyer. He was glad to be back at East Whittier Elementary School and quickly renewed his friendships among the students and teachers. He had a part in the annual eighth-grade play and, at graduation time, in 1926, he wrote the class history, was named the outstanding member of his class, and also had the honor of being the valedictorian.

Dick Nixon just naturally took to learning, although he had his positive likes and dislikes among his school subjects. Math and science were low on his list, but he still worked hard at them and earned good grades. "The best test of a man," he said years later, "is not how well he does the things he likes but how well he does the things he doesn't like."

For two years after graduation from elementary school, Dick quietly attended Fullerton Junior High School, located some miles south of Whittier. He stayed with his uncle Walter Nixon, one of his father's brothers, while at Fullerton. Since he was a newcomer who knew very few people in town, outside of his relatives, he was shy at first, but his debating coach helped him overcome this to such an extent that he eventually became known as a fine public speaker. As a freshman, he competed against upper classmen in a national oratorical contest sponsored by a Los Angeles newspaper. He was not too successful while a frosh, but during his sophomore year he won second place.

Dick did not play on any of the athletic teams at Fullerton but, because of his training on the violin, he was accepted by the school orchestra leader as a second violinist.

After his two years at Fullerton, Dick Nixon transferred to Whittier High School, which had a big, sprawling campus with handsome, Spanish-style buildings and broad, landscaped grounds. From 1928 to 1930, he went through two of the busiest years of his life. The Nixon Market was a great time-consumer, even without the service station, which had been leased to various individuals over the years, including Merle West, the cousin with whom Dick had grown up in Yorba Linda. Dick felt that he should help out in the store as often as possible in order to ease the pressure on his parents. His mother and father rose long before sunrise and worked eighteen hours a day to keep the market going. Hannah Nixon turned her skill in the kitchen into an economic asset and began each day by baking dozens of pies. This not only added nicely to the store's profits but it also was a means of using up the bruised fruit which could not be sold and which otherwise would have gone to waste. All three sons helped as much as they could. Dick took care of the produce stand as well as the accounts.

While he was family bookkeeper, Dick Nixon had a chance to see his parents' belief in the brotherhood of man put to the test. He saw the bills of families hit by illness or bad luck carried on the books sometimes for years. And in other ways, too, the Nixons showed compassion for people. One of the problems all storekeepers face is that of shoplifters. One day, when Dick was about fifteen, a woman told his mother that one of their best customers was regularly stealing from them. The Nixons were surprised, since they had known the accused woman for a long time and thought that she was perfectly honest. They watched her carefully after that until they were sure that she was a thief.

The family held a conference to decide on a course of action. Mrs. Nixon feared that arresting the shoplifter might damage her family in the eyes of the community, but Mr. Nixon felt that stealing was stealing and should be punished. What made it worse was that both of the woman's sons were friends of Richard and attended Sunday School with him. Dick saw the situation from a boy's point of view, arguing that the woman's arrest would scar his friends' lives forever. His arguments won over the harder line advocated by his father, and the family agreed to have Mrs. Nixon talk to the thief.

When caught in the act of hiding an item under her coat, the woman meekly confessed but begged Mrs. Nixon not to tell her husband. She promised to pay the debt off little by little. She eventually made restitution for all the goods stolen, which gave Mrs. Nixon and her son a great deal of satisfaction, since it proved that their policy of compassion had been successful.

It was difficult to have a close family life with the demands made on them all by the store, but the Nixons tried very hard to be together whenever the chance was offered. They always made sure to have breakfast together, so that they might say their morning prayers as a family. They continued their habit of regular church attendance. "We used to go to church four times a day on Sunday," Richard Nixon once said, "Sunday school, then church, then Christian education, then church in the evening." These habits of prayer and family closeness allowed the Nixons to give strength to each other after the death of Arthur, and it also fortified them for the next misfortune that befell them.

When Richard's older brother Harold was eighteen he came down with tuberculosis and began to suffer greatly from this dread disease. It was a desperate blow to the family, since, in addition to the deep concern they felt for the afflicted, it meant that everyone had to strain even harder to carry the load in the store. Doctors' bills mounted, but still Harold grew worse. His mother was faced with a hard decision. In order to do everything possible for Harold, she had taken him to a TB sanitarium, where she was advised that he should go to Arizona for the benefit of the dry air there. This would leave the rest of the family without anyone to run the household for them. The choice was a difficult one.

When it was suggested that Harold be put into a public

institution for tuberculosis sufferers, the Nixons refused, even though it meant breaking up the family and also increased debt. Reviewing his parents' decision years later, Richard Nixon observed: "They did not object to others receiving such help, but they felt strongly that those who were able to take care of themselves ought to make an all-out effort to do so."

Mrs. Nixon took Harold to the town of Prescott, Arizona, so that now the family had two households to manage. To solve the financial end of their problem, everyone had to sacrifice and work even harder. Mr. Nixon sold part of his property to a good family friend named Harry Schuyler, who paid for it by giving the Nixons eighty-five dollars a month. Hannah Nixon rented a house in Prescott and did her part by caring for several other young men who were afflicted as Harold was. There was nothing she did not do, from cooking and cleaning to washing the germ-laden clothing and bedding and emptying the bedpans. But what bothered her most was that all her efforts did not seem to help Harold, who grew progressively more ill and became more and more homesick.

Back at the market, Mr. Nixon, Richard, and Donald carried on as best they could. After school, the two boys put in hours of dull work, stacking cans on shelves, keeping the store clean, and doing all the dozens of jobs a shopkeeper must do. Since Nixon's Market stayed open until nine or ten o'clock at night, they ate dinner hurriedly, throwing together a meal of canned beans and hamburgers, chili, fried eggs, or spaghetti—just anything they could rustle up quickly. Sometimes, for breakfast, Richard grabbed only a candy bar.

It was in the midst of this uncertainty and confusion that Dick Nixon finished his last two years of high school. Far from being crushed by family troubles, however, he used his school hours to the fullest, engaging in many activities, perhaps because he was able to control these better than the outside forces. One of his classmates later compared him to a track runner who builds himself up as an athlete by competing against himself, setting tough personal goals and challenging himself to reach them. Dick tried to excel in studies, in public speaking, and any other activity he entered.

Dick's talent as a student was brought out at Whittier High School, where he earned top grades, including "A's" in Latin. To get these was not easy. He often had to study late into the night, working in the little tower of the converted meetinghouse which still served as the family store.

Dick improved as a speaker while at Whittier High. As a junior, in March of 1929, even though he was a new student, Dick represented his school in an oratorical contest and won ten dollars by defeating seventeen other contestants. The speech he made was on the Constitution of the United States and in it were reflected some of the ideas that Richard Nixon has held throughout his life. He reviewed the rights guaranteed by the Constitution: trial by jury, right to legal help, freedom of worship, freedom of speech, and freedom of the press. But he didn't stop there. He went on to emphasize the duties of the citizen, criticizing persons who have the right to vote but do not use it. "To use the ballot is the citizen's duty to himself, to his fellowmen, and to his country," he said. And he had even sterner words for those who abuse their other liberties, such as freedom of speech or the press:

> There are some who use them as a cloak for covering libelous, indecent and injurious statements against their fellowmen. Should the morals of this nation be offended and polluted in the name of freedom of speech or freedom of the press? In the words of Lincoln, the individual can have no rights against the best interests of society. Furthermore, there are those who, under the pretense of freedom of speech and freedom of the press, have incited riots, assailed our patriotism, and denounced the Constitution. Consequently, laws have justly been provided for punishing those who abuse their Constitutional privileges—laws which do not limit these privileges, but which provide that they may not be instrumental in destroying the Constitution which insures them.

This early speech illustrates three things about its author. First, Richard Nixon showed in it how deeply he felt about his country's highest law. His respect for it seemed almost like a religious feeling. This is a key to his later life, since he carried his veneration for the Constitution with him into public office. In addition, from his manner of expressing his ideals, he proved that he was already beginning to talk, write, and think as a lawyer does. Finally, it revealed his advanced understanding of legal principles, particularly the concepts that a nation has the right to protect itself from those who would use its own laws to destroy it, and that every legal right which man possesses has a duty accompanying it.

When he became an upperclassman at Whittier High and began to think about the possibilities of college, Dick was put in complete charge of the Nixon Market's produce counter. Although this offered him a source of income from which to save for tuition, it also gave him added responsibilities. Every morning, he was up before dawn and on his way to the Los Angeles markets in the family's battered pick-up truck. When he returned, he scrubbed the vegetables and fruit in back of the house. Then began the laborious task, still before school, of arranging his goods on the counter so that each showed to advantage. "I never pass a fruit market," Dick Nixon later said, "without thinking of the man who had to pick out the bad fruit and polish up the good and make the displays."

Even with his morning and afternoon duties at the store, Dick somehow found time for extra-curricular activities at Whittier High. He was on the staff of the school's weekly newspaper, was a member of the Latin Club, was president of the Scholarship Society, and, of course, was the school's champion debater. As a senior, Dick ran for the office of president of the student body, but was defeated in a three-man race. He was elected general manager of the student body, though, which was quite an honor for a transfer student.

In 1930, he won thirty dollars in prizes for an extemporaneous speech on "American Progress, Its Dependence Upon the Constitution." In this speech, he attributed the success of the United States to its governmental system under the Constitution. It was not, he said, because Americans were any kind of special race that they were successful; nor was it because they were blessed with great natural resources. They had become a great people because they had found the best way to govern themselves. Here, more of Richard Nixon's growing philosophy of government can be recognized.

During his senior year, Dick volunteered to act the leading role in a play put on by his Latin Club. He took the part of a Trojan hero, Aeneas, while a classmate named Ola Florence Welch played the heroine. The club members were dressed in Roman togas and ate Roman style at a banquet. Dick and Ola began dating at that time and remained close friends for years.

As graduation neared, Dick had to decide on his future course of action. There were many choices open to him. One of these was a chance to go to Harvard University, perhaps even on a scholarship. Harold's illness and Dick's desire to continue to help out at home were two strong reasons for his turning down this opportunity. Finally, he decided to apply to Whittier College, which his mother had attended, since this was close to home. He was accepted and even received some financial aid from a Milhous family fund to help defray tuition costs. This, plus what he still made on the fruit and vegetable counter, helped put him through college.

During the 1920's, the United States had experienced a period of great prosperity. At the end of the decade, however, a stock market crash occurred, resulting in a Depression which was beginning to be felt as Dick Nixon graduated from high school. In 1930, unemployment was well over four million persons, but by 1932, this would grow to twelve million unemployed. Misery was not slow in reaching Whittier, as the Nixons quickly discovered. The list of customers buying on credit began to swell, as did the length of time it took them to settle their accounts. Jobs became scarcer, wages and prices fell, and each month things seemed to be getting worse. Whittier was a "Republican" town, that is, most of the people in it voted Republican, but it was hard to have faith in President Herbert Hoover as the bottom kept dropping out of the country's economy.

Added to the national woes, the illness of Harold was constantly on the minds of each member of the Nixon family. During the time Mrs. Nixon and Harold spent in Prescott, Arizona, Frank Nixon tried to visit them as often as possible. On weekends he would take Dick and Don with him on the fifteen-hour auto trip across mountains and deserts. It was a real hardship and left everyone exhausted for the next few days, but the hours spent together were well worth the tremendous effort. During one summer vacation, Dick went to Prescott and obtained a temporary job as a "barker" at the Frontier Days Rodeo. But the presence of his mother and the visits of his father and brothers did not prevent Harold, who was a sensitive and poetic person, from feeling homesick. He finally prevailed upon his mother to return to Whittier. They did and the family was once more united, although Harold's condition was not improved.

One bright spot appeared in the midst of these troubles.

This was the birth in May, 1930, of Frank and Hannah Nixon's fifth and last child. Once again, it was a boy. He was named Edward Calvert Nixon. In several ways, Edward's birth gave new life to the Nixon family.

CHAPTER III

❧

Harold's illness, naturally, dampened the feeling of satisfaction and pride in the Nixon family over Dick's entry into college. But for Dick, the first weeks of the fall 1930 semester left him with little time to think of anything but his new school.

The Whittier campus was located on the edge of the town of Whittier itself, at the base of a small slope known as "college hill." Set among groves of fruit trees, the college consisted of only a few small buildings, serving a student body of four hundred members. The classrooms "were not particularly attractive," Richard Nixon said later. "They were crowded, they were most inadequate." But, he continued, the teachers they had were "magnificent; they were dedicated; they worked for less than they could get in similar activities and professions other than teaching and they left an indelible mark on those who came through those classrooms in that period."

The class of 1934 was not a big one—by graduation time, there were only eighty-five members. They grew to know one another pretty well during their four years together, and in some cases strong friendships resulted. A few of Richard Nixon's staunchest political supporters came from this class. Because he was well known and liked from high-school days by many of his college classmates, he had a built-in following or "constituency." He was elected fresh-man class president. Since he intended to prepare for a law career, he registered for the prescribed liberal arts course. He also signed up for three freshman athletic teams—track, football, and basketball. And, following his earlier interest, he became a member of the frosh debating team.

All this added up to an unusually full college program. When it was topped by his work in the family store, the sum of Dick Nixon's activities could almost be called fran-tic. Years later, his mother suggested that this schedule might be explained by Dick's desire to take his parents' minds off the loss of Arthur and the serious illness of Har-old. Perhaps it was to take *his* mind off the sorrow. Of course, it might have been that he was so brimming over with energy he just had to use it up in vigorous physical and mental exertion. His football coach later explained his activities by saying that Dick "just wanted to be in things." Whatever the reasons for his very full college life, Dick Nixon was "in" almost everything at Whittier.

He loved sports of all kinds. When he was younger, he had played sandlot baseball and soccer and had even laid out a tennis court with his brothers and friends in back of the store. In his first year of college, he put his heart into freshman sports, but unfortunately, his feet wouldn't obey him all of the time. He was slow on the track team, medi-ocre on the baseball field, and took part in every football game played by the frosh only because the team consisted of eleven men. He was enthusiastic, though, and a good team rooter.

Participating in sports was very important to Dick Nixon, even if he did not excel in them. He loved the competition, the challenge. In this, he was like one of his boyhood idols, Teddy Roosevelt, who had advocated the strenuous life as a character-builder.

Richard Nixon's membership on the debating team gave him the opportunity to tour the northwestern section of the United States with a teammate during the Christmas vacation of 1930. They covered 3500 miles. This travel was a broadening experience, as was the study necessary in preparation for the debates. Tariff and trade were the topics selected because these were important factors in American life in 1930, as they are today.

Supplementing his debating activity was his continued interest in dramatics. Richard Nixon realized that a public speaker—or a lawyer—cannot get his message across if he merely recites facts. He must be able to present his case dramatically, with the proper gestures and voice techniques. By participating in the freshman play at college, he gained what he felt was valuable experience as a character actor.

During this same year, he also played the piano for religious services at East Whittier Friends church and taught Sunday School. He worked on the Whittier College yearbook, wrote for the school newspaper, and participated in an extemporaneous speaking contest sponsored by the *Reader's Digest*. This was a grueling but exciting challenge, since the judges were free to choose any one of many articles appearing in the magazine and the candidate was expected to remember the substance of the piece and present it in a fresh and original way. Between debating, dramatics, and extemporaneous speaking, freshman Nixon did a lot of fast thinking and talking on his feet.

The Quaker founders of Whittier College wanted to avoid some of the social problems of other colleges and so forbade fraternities and sororities on the campus. In this way, they hoped to discourage snobbishness among their students. But since young people in schools naturally form little cliques, it is difficult to outlaw all campus social groups. There were several girls' clubs and one society for the boys, known as the Franklins.

Although some of his friends joined, membership in the Franklins did not appeal to Dick Nixon, since the society was considered to be somewhat stuffy and complacent. When an older friend suggested that a new social group be started, Dick jumped at the idea and threw himself into helping to organize it with great enthusiasm. The new outfit was named the Orthogonians, from the Greek words meaning "square shooters." In order to show the Franklins that they were easy-going, the Orthogonians wore floppy sweaters with big "O's" on them. Their motto was "Beans, Brawn, Brains, and Bowels," and they had their own song, written by Richard Nixon, in honor of the animal they took as their symbol—the boar. It began:

> All hail the mighty boar
> Our patron beast is he
> Our aims forevermore
> In all our deeds must be

To emulate his might
His bravery and his fight. . . .

The poetry and logic were terrible, but the spirit was
strong.

The Orthogonians attracted all types of persons but had
a special appeal for the athletes, and the group soon became
noted for boosting school athletic activities. A feature of the
club was the monthly spaghetti and beans feed, held in a
local restaurant. Once in a while, Grandmother Milhous
would have the whole gang over to her big house for a roast
lamb feast. Perhaps because he was one of the "founding
fathers," composed the club song, helped write its constitution, and recruited many members, Dick was elected first
president of the Orthogonians.

The friendly rivalry between Franklins and Orthogonians
was not serious and rarely came to the surface except when
either side sponsored candidates for school offices. Then,
the Franklins were depicted as rich, well-dressed, literary
types, stuffed shirts who felt they were better than anyone
else. And the Orthogonians were considered unkempt slobs,
with poor taste in clothes and clubs.

Actually, all the students at Whittier College were pretty
much on equal terms socially and financially. One member
of the Franklins worked as a part-time janitor and lived in
a small room under the gymnasium, while another earned his
tuition by digging ditches and waiting on tables. One Orth-
ogonian was a "soda jerk," while another, named Clint
Harris, cleaned chicken coops to help pay for his college
education. Clint, who was one of Dick Nixon's football
teammates, also worked as a citrus-grove sprayer, earning

eight dollars a night for this back-breaking labor. Not all jobs paid this well, however, and most students had to be content with thirty-five cents an hour for their services.

Meals could be purchased in local boardinghouses for a quarter, and tuition for the entire school year was only $250. Almost everyone had some kind of job. Some worked on their parents' farms or in fruit-packing plants, or, as was the case with Dick Nixon, in the family business. It was a time when money was scarce and many a student was grateful for the chance to pick a couple of avocados off the trees growing on campus to serve as lunch. If tuition was too high to pay in cash, the college would accept farm produce— even in the form of manure for fertilizing—instead.

Students at Whittier College took their class work very seriously, partly because of their home training and partly because most of them were working so hard to earn their tuition. They also knew how difficult it would be, later on, to get a job in Depression-torn America. During the years when Dick Nixon attended college, from 1930 to 1934, unemployment was higher than it had been in any period in American history, so a thorough education was most important.

Work they certainly did! Examinations, term papers, extra readings—it seemed that it was just one learning hurdle after another. Even Dick Nixon, who waded into work the way a surfer rushes into the waves, was sometimes depressed by it all. "Could it be possible," he asked, in a piece written for the school newspaper, "that the college student is attempting to cram too much knowledge into his head during the space of four years? Surely there are times when the great amount of outside reading, extra work, and long assignments become such a drudgery to the student that he cannot separate the most important material from the unimportant."

But if Dick Nixon thought college was a tough grind, he did not slow down as he entered sophomore year. He was elected to an office in student government, once again toured the Pacific Northwest as a debater, and turned out for the varsity football team. In this last activity, he was in over his head. At a weight of only about 150 pounds, he was like a feather to his teammates. He almost never got to play in the games, but he never missed practice. No one could understand why he kept coming back for more. He was always in the thick of the scrimmage, getting spread all over the field by his huskier teammates. "We were cannon fodder," said one of Dick's friends, who also sat on the bench most of the time. Dick always said he didn't mind warming the bench, though, because it gave him a seat on the fifty-yard line.

Nixon's desire to be on the team, even though he was not a first stringer, was well known to the small student body. So when old "23" (his jersey number) did get his rare chance to play, an extra cheer would go up from the friendly Whittier rooters. Dick would have his brief moment of enthusiastic glory . . . then the coach would yank him back to the bench.

Football taught Dick Nixon the absolute need for self-discipline and rigorous training. It also gave him the friendship of some fine, hard-working fellow-players—and it brought him under the guidance of "Chief" Newman, the football coach.

Wallace Newman, nicknamed "Chief" by his friends because of his Indian ancestry, exerted an important influence on Dick Nixon. Raised among his own people until he was nineteen, Chief Newman spent the rest of his life among whites. He was a husky, strapping man, a good football player himself while in college, and he had the knack of recognizing talent when he saw it—and that included more than athletic prowess. Dick Nixon may not have been a very skillful player but he had pluck—and he was also the best team booster, following every play and cheering the team on in victory and defeat. "I was a lousy football player," he admitted years later, but Chief Newman could add, "He came in with all the enthusiasm in the world."

One of the things about Dick Nixon that most impressed his football teammates was his willingness to visit local high schools, to speak at rallies on behalf of Whittier College. Although he was awkward on the football field, he handled himself well when speaking to large gatherings of students, "selling" them on his school in a funny, easy-going way.

Dick's studies, work at the store, and extra-curricular activities went a long way toward lightening some of the burden of sadness over the loss of Arthur and the continuing illness of Harold. And Edward was helping a little to fill the place left empty by Arthur's death.

Dick did not have any close girl friends at this time. He was rather shy around girls and hesitant about asking for dates, so, when there was a party for couples, he usually took his high-school friend, Ola Florence Welch, who was also attending Whittier College with him. He found it easy to do things with Ola Florence because she seemed more like a familiar old friend than a formal date. Ola Florence loved to discuss politics with Dick because of his intense loyalty to his father's Republican heroes, while she was a Democrat and supported President Franklin D. Roosevelt. Ola and Dick could argue heatedly and yet remain on good terms.

While at college, Dick Nixon had the opportunity to check some of his father's views. Among the persons the latter respected highly in American life, besides William McKinley, were Teddy Roosevelt and a Wisconsin reformer named Robert LaFollette. Frank Nixon was a progressive type of Republican. He believed the party should stand for worthwhile reform and, when he thought it did not, it lost his support. In fact, he voted for Franklin D. Roosevelt in 1936.

Surveys show that most people vote the way their parents do, at least when they first begin their lives as citizens. If they belong to a political party, they automatically vote for its nominees. Frank Nixon was never this kind of a party member and he wanted his children to think for themselves, too. At college, through his own study and personal observation, Dick came to accept the majority of his father's views on politics, only now this was more the outcome of his independent reading and checking than family loyalty.

Dick trusted his father's judgment in many things. Sometimes Mr. Nixon would drive the Whittier debating team to nearby colleges for competitions. He would join the audience for the entire debate, listening to the arguments and weighing their values. On the way home, he would take the performances apart and give pointers on them. Frank Nixon was not noted for the correctness of his speech, but if there was one thing he knew, it was the fine points of argumentation.

Dick Nixon's father was the man who influenced him most in his life. Next came his football coach, Chief Wallace Newman, and Paul Smith, a brilliant historian and teacher at Whittier. Later, Dr. Smith became president of the college, a post he held for many years.

Dr. Smith was typical of the type of teacher who was attracted to Whittier College. He had excellent intellectual and teaching qualifications for his job, but more than this, he made the campus his life, staying around after classes to discuss things with his students, playing horeshoes with them and giving them more than just a fine classroom performance. Dr. Smith and the other members of the faculty loved their school so much that they took a 25 per cent salary cut to keep it from going out of business during the Depression. One year, the college paid its faculty in the form of parcels of land near the campus. Despite the hardships, many of the teachers stayed on and found their commitment rewarded by the respect their students gave to them and to their ideas.

Richard Nixon became a history major and took many courses with Dr. Smith. He studied American and British history, constitutional theory, historical methods, and international relations. Under Dr. Smith's influence, Dick Nixon came to see that history was shaped by the great men of the past. This "great man" theory of history is one of the most popular ways of explaining past events. In discussing such men as Abraham Lincoln and James Madison, Dr. Smith taught his students that "a good president is one who perceives the popular will and executes it." Richard Nixon read very widely during this period of his life. He became familiar not only with the standard works of history but he also read the works of Tolstoy, Rousseau, and Voltaire.

Dick Nixon's seemingly boundless energy was the envy of his classmates. He continued to take piano lessons, this time from a music professor at the college, who thought he was a "careful piano student," playing the works of Brahms especially well. Dick also sang in the Whittier College Glee Club. But of all these extra activities, the most important to him was dramatics, in which he participated with great enthusiasm, under the able guidance of Professor Albert Upton, the head of the English Department. Professor Upton spent hours coaching the young Whittier Thespians. For an amateur actor, Dick turned in good performances, playing an old man in one production and learning how to "cry" in another.

On the stage and in the classroom, Dick Nixon managed to feel sure of himself without being cocky. When he disagreed with a professor, he did not hesitate to say so, engaging in a man-to-man debate which won the admiration of his classmates. They knew that this was not "showing off" but was rather part of Dick's inquiring nature. He was too serious to "show off." As one of his classmates put it, he was the "type of fellow who would be on time even if the boss was on vacation."

When the local Rotary Club, an association of businessmen, asked for a student speaker from Whittier College, Dick was delegated to go. The president of the club remembered later that Dick Nixon delivered an earnest speech in which he said that more young people should get into politics. As it turned out, he was the only one out of his college class who did take up a political career.

Dick's junior year at college was as active as the previous two had been. He served as student body vice president and continued his debating activity with a 3000-mile tour of Arizona, Nevada, Utah, Oregon, and other states. This traveling, which most college students are not fortunate enough to manage, was a valuable experience for Richard Nixon. Instead of being rooted in just one area because of lack of funds, he had the opportunity to meet students with varied backgrounds over ranges of thousands of miles, seeing their local ways of solving problems and their individual manner of living.

It was an active year for him dramatically, too. He appeared in two productions, in one of which he took the lead opposite Ola Florence Welch. He also served as stage manager for another play. In 1933, he bought his first car, a 1930 Ford Model A, for $300. His cousin, Merle West, who knew a great deal about cars, went with him to buy it, to help him pick out a good one. Machinery was never a strong point with Richard Nixon.

As Dick's junior year rolled toward the spring of 1933, the tragedy that had long been hovering over the family became a reality. The return of Harold to Whittier had brought no improvement in his tubercular condition. Instead, his illness became more and more serious. Early in March, as Mrs.

Nixon's birthday was approaching, Harold asked Dick to drive him to a store where he could buy a present for her. Harold chose an electric cake mixer to make it easier for his mother to bake. Dick dropped him off at home, then headed for college. Shortly after he reached there, he received word that Harold was dead. Of the five Nixon boys, only Dick, Donald, and two-year-old Edward remained.

After the funeral, Dick plunged into work with his usual great energy. He decided to run for president of the student body for the forthcoming senior year at college. This activity helped him to handle his grief better, and helped take the family's mind off their loss. His opponent was a likable, easy-going student named Dick Thomson, a member of the Franklins. Dick had the Orthogonians behind him and he was able to make his campaign very lively. One of the issues was whether dancing should be permitted on campus. Whittier was a traditional Friends' school and its leading administrators and trustees were determined to keep it that way. Drinking was not allowed and students who wished to smoke went off campus. Card playing and other forms of gambling were discouraged. Naturally, the suggestion that dancing be permitted was a radical proposal.

Dick Thomson fought hard, but Dick Nixon had the popular issue and he was also a better speaker. Thomson, in fact, later modestly said that he "felt like a blubbering idiot against a silver-tongued orator." Whatever the reason, Richard Nixon became student body president for his senior year. And his grieving parents did take some comfort in his success. He kept his campaign promise, persuading the Board of Trustees to relax the bann on dancing by arguing that, if they did not, the students might only go off campus and perhaps get into trouble in Los Angeles.

"President Nixon has literally worked his head off lately . . . ," wrote one of the editors of the Whittier College newspaper to describe Dick's efforts as student-body president. Another of his accomplishments was to start a big weekend festival, to be shared in by everyone on campus. This included dancing, picnicking, and competitive games. He also launched the practice of including the officers elected for the following year in the planning and discussions that went on during the last months of their predecessors' terms in office. This gave them a chance to see what was in store for them when they took over and to build their plans accordingly.

Dick continued his dramatic work while a senior, appearing in two productions and playing the lead in one of them. He won a local contest for extemporaneous speaking, continued as a member of the debating team, and still managed to maintain high grades.

Added to the anticipation of graduation from college was the happy news that Dick had been granted a tuition scholarship to the Duke University Law School. This award was worth $250 a year, a sizable amount in Depression-torn America, when college graduates were taking jobs at eighteen to twenty dollars a week. Still, the scholarship did not cover board, transportation, clothing, and other expenses. In addition, this was a very competitive grant. Duke University was a large institution located in Durham, North Carolina. It was just starting its law school and, to attract the best students from around the country, it was very gen-

Richard Nixon

White House Photos

Hannah Milhous and Frank Nixon, Richard Nixon's parents, were married in 1908.

White House Photos

Frank Nixon in 1907 when he worked for the Pacific Electric Railway as a motorman between Los Angeles and Whittier.

Barefoot boys—Harold Nixon and little brother Richard in Yorba Linda

Frank and Hannah Nixon, Harold, Richard, and Donald.
Richard (right) was three years old at the time.

LEFT: An early portrait of Richard Nixon, taken about 1916

RIGHT: The Nixon boys at Yorba Linda—Richard, 9, is standing at left, then Harold, 12, Arthur, 4, and Donald, 7, is in the tire. Another brother, Edward, was born in 1930.

Richard Nixon is at far right of the first row in this picture taken at the Yorba Linda school. Many of the students were barefoot.

Photo Trends

BELOW LEFT: The Anaheim Ditch is empty and dry today, but when the Nixon boys lived in Yorba Linda the water that rushed through the cement trough close to their home was a constant worry to their mother. RIGHT: The birthplace of Richard Nixon in Yorba Linda, California, as it looks today.

Author's Collection

White House Photos

ABOVE: The Nixon boys in 1923—Harold in a Scout hat, Arthur who was the youngest at that time, Donald, and Richard. The girls are unidentified.

RIGHT: Richard Nixon at about ten years of age. The Nixons moved to Whittier in 1922.

White House Photos

Arthur's seventh birthday—Richard and Donald are in the back row. Arthur (left) died shortly after.

White House Photos

White House Photos

East Whittier School, 1926. Richard Nixon is fourth from the left in the back row.

Richard Nixon with his mother and Donald on East Whittier Boulevard, 1926

White House Photos

Richard Nixon played second violin with the high school orchestra at Fullerton.

A photo from the Whittier High School yearbook. Richard Nixon, a junior, placed first and won a prize of ten dollars for his speech on the Constitution in March, 1929.

Both: White House Photos

The three Nixon boys in 1929, Richard, Harold, and Donald

Richard Nixon was elected general manager of the student body in his senior year at Whittier High.

Both: White House Photos

STUDENT BODY OFFICERS

Richard Nixon
General Manager

Robert Logue
President

Ralph Garman
Vice President

Dorothy Petty
Secretary-Treasurer

White House Photos

Harold and Richard Nixon with two unidentified girls about 1930

A view of the family market, taken long after Richard ran the produce counter. The Nixon boys all worked in the family market at one time. Edward is shown here in the left background, grinding up hamburger. George Brickles, a cousin, is at the vegetable department and George Irving in the meat department.

White House Photos

Richard Nixon and Ola Florence Welch dated during high school days.

Richard Nixon (#12 here) participated in football throughout his four years at Whittier College. He spent most of the Varsity years on the bench, but played all his freshman games because there were only eleven men on the squad.

White House Photos

Richard Nixon with his younger brother Edward at Long Beach, California

OPPOSITE: When her grandson graduated from law school, Grandmother Almira Milhous, then eighty-eight years old, insisted on taking the long, cross-country drive to his graduation. Here she is shown with Frank, Hannah, and Edward Nixon in front of the Duke University Chapel.

White House Photos

Richard Nixon's class at law school, Duke University

White House Photos

To Mother
with Love
from Dick· 1935

erous with first-year scholarships. If Dick did not maintain high grades, however, he would not be eligible for renewal in his second and third years.

In spite of these drawbacks, the day in May, 1934, when Dick heard the good news was one of the happiest in his life. This was the beginning of the realization of a dream he had held since he was a small boy worried over the scandals which had marred the Presidential administration of Warren Harding. Then, according to family accounts, Dick Nixon had pledged himself to become an honest lawyer, satisfying his Quaker sense of mission in that manner.

Besides the direct aid which the scholarship meant for him, it had other meanings, too. It was a great honor to receive such an award and it was nice to know how the officials of Whittier College felt about him. He could not help being proud of a letter of recommendation from the president of his college which had helped to gain the scholarship for him. Dr. Walter Dexter wrote that he thought Richard Nixon would become "one of America's important, if not great leaders."

Of course, there were still obstacles to be surmounted, such as where Dick would get the remaining money needed for his board and transportation. His family solved this by promising to help him out and, on the strength of the glowing letter by President Dexter, the Dean of the Duke Law School offered him a part-time job. Now, all that remained for Dick to do was to take his final exams—and enjoy the remainder of his last college semester.

Graduation day dawned, clear and beautiful, and the exercises were conducted outside, under the brilliant California sun and in sight of the majestic mountains which rise just at the southeastern end of the town of Whittier. Richard Nixon graduated second in his class. He was topped by Regina Dunkin, who took highest honors and was class valedictorian.

While Richard Nixon was working his way through college, Patricia Ryan was growing up, burdened by hardships, in the nearby town of Artesia. Her father died of silicosis, a lung disease from which miners often suffer, when she was only seventeen and had just graduated from high school. This, added to the death of her mother five years earlier, was a near-crushing blow, at first. But Pat was a courageous person who refused to stay down for very long. She took a job in a bank, working as a teller. When she heard that several elderly friends were traveling by car to the East Coast and needed a driver, she offered her services. It was a tough trip, and Pat had her hands full, changing flat tires and trying to work the car's creaky brake system.

She went to New York and secured a job in a hospital, while she studied radiology at Columbia University. Becoming an x-ray technician, she worked at this for a few years before returning to California.

Pat Ryan was very ambitious and determined. The daughter of hard-working parents who had not had much schooling, she had grown up with an urge to obtain as much of an education as she possibly could.

Back on the West Coast, Patricia Ryan entered the University of Southern California (or USC), one of the best-known schools in the country. She studied business subjects, intending to work in a department store eventually as a buyer or in some executive position. She always had to work to support herself while in college, and held a number of interesting jobs—in a department store, as a secretary, and even as a Hollywood movie extra, at the coaxing of her friends. A beautiful girl with reddish hair, handsome features, and a fine, proud bearing, she certainly looked like a movie star. She earned as much as seven dollars a day for her work as an extra. She even had a line to deliver in one movie and was paid twenty-five dollars for it!

But Hollywood was not for Pat Ryan. When she graduated from USC with honors, she received an offer of a teaching post in Whittier High School. The pay was very good—over forty dollars a week. She couldn't resist this so, instead of heading toward a department store, she was soon on her way to the serene atmosphere of the Quaker town.

In the autumn of 1934, Richard Nixon took up his studies on the campus of Duke University in North Carolina. For the next three years, he had the opportunity to observe life in the South at close range, just as he had been able to see the West as a member of the debating team while in college.

His family sent him thirty-five dollars a month for food and lodging. This sum was augmented by occasional gifts from Grandmother Almira Milhous and his aunt, Edith Timberlake. To keep expenses down, Dick did not live in a dormitory on campus. For a short time, he stayed in a rooming house but found he could not concentrate on his studying with all the noise there, so he and three classmates decided to share a place. About a mile from Duke was an old farmhouse owned by a lady who lived there with her child. She rented the four students a room with two double beds and an old stove for a few dollars a month each.

They gave their new home the high-sounding title of "Whippoorwill Manor," but it really was a ramshackle place, with no running water and a poor heating system which was of little help to them in the winter. But Dick and his three companions were all healthy young men and they figured out ways to beat the disadvantages. They shaved and showered in the school's facilities, hiding their shaving equipment behind books in the library.

One of Dick's friends bought an old Packard for forty dollars and that provided transportation for the group. They used it to drive to a local boardinghouse, where the landlady served them all they could eat for twenty-five cents per meal.

Attending law school is, in itself, a difficult task. Hours of reading are required each day and careful notes must be taken in class so that legal points and principles are not overlooked. Dick found it hard holding down the part-time job he had in the library and competing with the other eager students whom the Law School had attracted through its generous scholarships.

Dick had always been a serious person, and law school seemed to make him even more serious. He studied with an iron determination and passed his courses with high grades, but he was always worried, sure that he might be beaten out by other students. As a result, he was given the nickname "Gloomy Gus" by his classmates. He usually rose an hour or more earlier than his roommates every day to get in some extra studying. Actually, he had little reason to be gloomy. He proved to be an excellent law student, and his scholarship was renewed for the next two years.

Dick had little time for fun at Duke. Besides, he had been brought up to regard such activities as card playing and dancing as rather frivolous. He went on dates once in a while, enjoyed the rare beer parties, and took part in the horseplay and kidding common to all campuses. On one occasion, he and several other students sneaked into the Dean's office to find out their grades in a course.

Dick's most consistent outside interest while at law school was the Duke football team. One of his classmates said he was the "most enthusiastic rooter in school," willing to scream himself hoarse for the squad. He also went to church regularly while at Duke, either to the Chapel on campus or to a neighboring house of worship.

One break from the law-school grind came when Dick and several other students decided to take a winter trip to New York City. His brother Donald, who was attending Guilford College in North Carolina, conducted by the Society of Friends, also went along. The drive through dangerous winter weather had little effect on the exuberant spirits of the vacationers.

Dick's professors were quick to recognize his abilities as a student. He was selected to write several articles for the Duke law journal, a great honor for any future lawyer. His classmates respected him to the point of electing him president of the law-school student body in his senior year. And because he was in the top 10 per cent of his class, he was elected to the Order of the Coif, a national law fraternity.

Richard Nixon had taken up the law because he thought it would help him to serve mankind while, at the same time, it would provide him with a good living. As usual, he took his law seriously, discussing points and arguing cases with his teachers and fellow students on the basis of principles. He brought his strong Quaker beliefs with him to North Carolina and did not hesitate to stand up for them whenever he felt they were threatened. He was shocked by the way the Negro was treated in the South, for example, and he was quick to tell his Southern friends how he felt about this. He also got a taste of what law was like in action by working in a legal clinic, where he was required to gather facts for the local district attorney in Durham as part of a course he was taking. This involved him with people *and* the law and was the best sort of preparation for his chosen future career.

In spite of being so very busy, Richard Nixon often grew homesick for California and he wrote pretty regularly to his family and friends. Grandmother Milhous still kept up her practice of sending notes and money to her many grandchildren. Her pride in Richard was very great and led her to insist that she be included in the party when the Nixon family drove to Durham for Dick's graduation. Although they had their doubts about it, because she was then eighty-eight years old, Frank and Hannah Nixon couldn't say no, so they packed her with young Edward into their trusty Chevrolet and took the 3000-mile trip across country. She enjoyed the trip thoroughly, especially when her grandson graduated with honors, third in his class.

Richard Nixon was now twenty-three years old and he

had been going to school for the last eighteen years of his life. It was time to get to the business of making a living. It was something to which he could look forward, but it was also a cause for worry.

CHAPTER IV

✺

RICHARD NIXON and his fellow students had been in college and law school during seven hard Depression years, 1930 to 1937. But the year after they graduated things grew even worse and the country slid rapidly into a second Depression. In 1937, 7,700,000 Americans were jobless. By 1938, this number would rise to 10,400,000 before beginning to shrink.

Of course, Richard Nixon was luckier than most young people of his day. He had an excellent education and was the proud possessor of a law degree. But even this did not guarantee him a job. He had to hunt for one just as hard as anyone else. Before he left North Carolina, he went to New York City, where the most successful offices were located. His search was fruitless; there was no opening for him there. He applied for a position with the Federal Bureau of Investigation, passed the written examination, and was approved after a thorough investigation of his background. However, he was not appointed as an agent because a need to reduce expenses forced the FBI to cut back on hiring.

When he did secure a position, it was with Whittier's oldest law firm, Wingert and Bewley, headed by Thomas

Bewley. Tom Bewley was a well-known citizen in Whittier, a Friend whose grandfather had once been the business partner of Franklin Milhous, Dick's grandfather, back in Indiana. Dick's desk was prepared for him. All he needed to do was to pass the California State bar examination. The bar exam is extremely difficult to pass. Even after three years of law school, most prospective lawyers take an intensive "cram course," in which they review everything they have learned about the law. These courses are offered by special schools or are conducted by men who are already lawyers. Dick buckled down under the guidance of a brilliant and kindly blind lawyer from Los Angeles named Lloyd Nix. By iron determination, Richard Nixon crowded the work of months into a few strenuous weeks. When the bar examination results were announced, he was one of those who passed. More than 50 per cent of those who took the test failed.

A full-fledged lawyer now, Richard Nixon was able to take his place in his firm's office on the sixth floor of the Bank of America Building in the center of town. His secretary, a Canadian-born friend named Evelyn Dorn, later recalled approvingly that, on his first day on the job, attorney Richard Nixon rolled up his sleeves and spent his time in the dusty law library. Shelves were cleaned, books were dusted, and the entire place tidied up so well that it looked as neat as any corner in the Nixon Market. Then, the new lawyer began to show his employer the training that had won him honors in law school.

Many people think of a lawyer as an adventurous and superactive man, half detective, half crusader. There are some lawyers like that in real life but most exist only as the heroes in TV shows or mystery stories. The majority of attorneys, particularly the young ones, spend their time reading law books to find precedents, that is, the decisions in earlier cases, which might help the firm in arguing for its clients.

Dick Nixon characteristically began his law career by working sixteen hours a day, grinding out the legal arguments called briefs for his firm. Here the practice he had started in college of writing precisely came in handy. He rarely stopped, pausing only to send Mrs. Dorn out for hamburgers, milk shakes, or Mexican food as he worked on these briefs through his lunch and dinner hours. He threw himself wholeheartedly into law, as he had into every previous work or school experience.

While the young lawyer was becoming more familiar with legal work, Mr. Bewley invited him to observe cases being tried in court. Dick took notes on arguments for both sides, sized up the reactions of juries, and weighed the testimony of witnesses as if he were the one trying the case.

Tom Bewley's firm was a very conservative one. He tried to avoid court action if possible, because this was an expensive and time-consuming operation which rarely satisfied either party. The firm specialized for the most part in wills, corporation law, oil leases, and other aspects of business law.

Once in a while, Wingert and Bewley had to handle a divorce case and this chore went to the junior lawyer. Dick Nixon held to the belief that family harmony should be maintained at almost any cost. When clients came to him seeking divorces, he worked especially hard to help them reconcile their differences.

The great advantage of a small law office was that it gave a young attorney the opportunity to participate directly in many phases of the law, rather than being forced to specialize in just one aspect from the beginning. Dick Nixon came to know something of the laws governing federal taxes, estates of deceased clients, and business transactions. He even became involved in criminal law for a time. As a sideline, Tom Bewley was the official lawyer for the Whittier town government. He named Richard Nixon his assistant. This meant that Dick handled some of the duties which a full-time district attorney would perform in a large city. He prosecuted law breakers, such as persons who made nuisances of themselves by drinking too much in local restaurants, as well as handling other routine trial matters for the town.

When a case did go to trial, Dick Nixon was often the man who carried the ball. The experience he gained in watching the head of his firm in action, together with his special skill in debating and public speaking, made him a strong courtroom man. He prepared each brief with painstaking care, eager to leave nothing out as he followed the most difficult legal points through their intricate pathways.

Within a year, the firm was called Wingert, Bewley, and Nixon, as Dick was made a partner. In addition to his Whittier duties, he handled the firm's business in a branch office in nearby La Habra and was even named La Habra's official attorney. During the four years that he practiced law in Whittier, from 1937 to 1941, he became one of the rising young men of the community. His earnings as a lawyer reached six thousand dollars a year, a sizable sum for the nineteen-thirties. Older residents of the town proudly pointed out the handsome young lawyer in the neat blue suit as he strode quickly to his office and reminded their children that this was the boy who had once waited on them in the Nixon Market.

One big reason why Richard Nixon was held in such great respect by the citizens of Whittier was his willingness to give himself to every worthy cause. He became a member of the Whittier "20-30" Club, which consisted of young, community-minded persons in the town. He was elected president of the organization for one term and threw his support behind the group's aim to foster better local government. He was also president of the Junior Chamber of Commerce.

The fact that Richard Nixon returned to Whittier after law school and started his career in his home town was important to his future life. His many relatives and the friends with whom he grew up were very helpful to him. Many of them would become staunch political supporters in his later life. Of course, it was also a pleasure to be home once again with his mother and father and two brothers. He and Don, who was less than two years younger, were extremely close, going on vacations together and confiding in each other. Edward, now a grammar school boy, occupied a special place in his older brother's heart. Dick checked his homework and encouraged him to study hard.

Dick Nixon had a special knack for making friends from every age and level of life. Because he was willing to give a great deal of loyalty, he was usually rewarded with loyalty in return. Of course, this did not make him so very unusual. There were thousands of young men just like him in America at this time.

Richard Nixon was a born teacher, even though he might not have recognized it fully. During this period of his life, he taught Sunday School for his church. He also conducted a course at Whittier College in the application of law to practical problems. And when he was counseling couples on giving their marriages a chance to work, he really was also teaching.

His interest in education was rewarded when his "Alma Mater," Whittier College, named him to be a member of the Board of Trustees. At the age of twenty-six, he was the youngest member of the board. And when certain problems arose in the administration of the school, he was even briefly considered for the presidency.

These many and diverse activities could not consume all of Dick Nixon's energy, however. Looking around for something profitable to do, he joined a group of Whittier men who were seriously considering something they had always taken for granted—oranges. They decided to try to find a means of bringing orange juice to the breakfast table frozen in its freshly squeezed state. A company was established with Richard Nixon as president and chief attorney. But it was less of a solid business venture than a risky plunge by a group of friends who did most of their own work and took most of the risk. The new partners would head for the "plant" after working in their regular jobs and spend hours experimenting with processes for quick-freezing whole orange juice.

The business failed and the investors lost some ten thousand dollars on the enterprise. It was a big disappointment to all concerned, but particularly to Dick because he had been head of the outfit.

For Dick Nixon, life in the late 1930's seemed to offer about everything for which a young man could wish. He had a satisfying and well-paying career, he was active in the community, he was highly respected by friends and acquaintances, and to top it off, all was going well with his family. His mother and father were healthy, enjoyed a modest living from the Nixon Market, and were particularly proud of their three sons.

Yet, something was missing.

Patricia Ryan never regretted her decision to become a teacher in Whittier. Her arrival at the staid old school added a pleasant touch of color, youth, and beauty to the faculty. She involved herself wholeheartedly in her work, teaching typing and other business subjects to five classes of teen-age girls. Day after day, she faced her students with the same warm concern for them, pointing out mistakes and offering sensible advice to budding secretaries. But she always kept part of herself to herself and, in this way, seemed to some of her pupils to be a little reserved and stand-offish.

Her background fascinated the students—former movie actress, yet an honor student in college; a farm girl from nearby Artesia, yet one who had traveled across the entire United States and worked in New York City; a beautiful strawberry blonde in her twenties, yet not married. This was enough to keep a school full of normal girls and boys intrigued for years.

Pat had always loved to work—it gave meaning to her life, whether she was digging in the soil as a young farm girl, selling goods in a department store, or covering herself with ink while demonstrating the way to change a typewriter ribbon. She tried to impart this attitude toward work to her students—to make them respect their future positions as secretaries and stenographers. She also urged her classes to be neat and trim in their work and in their dress, setting the example herself.

Even while she kept possession of her personal independence, Pat Ryan had the rare gift of being friendly to everyone, students and teachers alike. And she was well liked in return. She served on planning committees for worthy causes, shared in faculty dinners of rabbit and other inexpensive foods fairly regularly, and took part in amateur theatrical performances. Pat's enthusiasm for working with young people led her to join other teachers in taking on all kinds of extra-curricular activities. They planned interesting assembly programs, shared in the fun of decorating for dances and sports activities, and cheered the teams as enthusiastically as any of the students did.

It was while she was engaged in one of her preferred activities—amateur dramatics—that she met Richard Nixon.

In the winter of 1938, Dick Nixon was a young man in his middle twenties who was inclined to spend his evenings poring over law books while many of his friends and schoolmates were marrying and beginning to raise families. He had dated quite a few girls, but none of them seemed to be the right match for him. He and Ola Florence Welch, whom he had dated while in high school and college, drifted apart in the years following college graduation, although they did correspond while Dick was in law school. Ola Florence married a man named Gail Jobe.

Perhaps Dick had not looked very seriously for a girl because he was so engrossed in getting his career started. His biggest social outlet was amateur theatricals and, since his return to Whittier from law school, he had been in several plays, once portraying a district attorney, a part in which he was then engaged in real life. The next production scheduled by his theater group was *The Dark Tower*. Dick became more interested than usual when he heard that there was a good-looking schoolteacher coming for try-outs.

So far, Dick Nixon had been a long-time planner, a methodical type of person who liked to think things through. But the first night he met Pat Ryan, he proposed to her—at least according to one account. Pat was interested in him but she was very surprised at such an impetuous gesture. Besides, she was not quite ready to get married. She suggested that they should get to know one another better before reaching such an important decision.

So, instead of marrying right away, the pair dated for two long years. They saw each other often, dining out together, taking long walks in the country, going places with their friends. Pat visited the Nixon home frequently and was a welcome guest. She grew especially close to Dick's mother, whom she helped in the store from time to time.

Hannah and Frank Nixon gave a big engagement party for Patricia Ryan and their son. The couple was married on June 21, 1940, at the Mission Inn in the town of Riverside, California. They drove off to Mexico City for their honeymoon. To reduce expenses, they took canned foods with them, but this produced some unusual combinations at mealtime, since their friends removed the labels from all the cans as a parting honeymoon gesture!

Although that June of 1940 brought special happiness to Pat and Dick Nixon, on the world scene, things were pretty bleak. Japanese aggression against China continued to occupy the headlines in the Pacific news, while the tragic fall of France to Hitler's Germany, only a day after Dick and Pat were married, was the main story from Europe. Still, it was necessary to go on living, and Europe and Asia seemed very far away from the newlyweds.

On returning from their honeymoon, the young couple made their home in a small apartment over a garage in Whittier. Both went back to work, their goal being to raise enough money to buy a house for the family they hoped to have. They joined their friends for amusements often, including ice skating in a newly opened rink. Like many Canadians, Evelyn Dorn was an excellent skater. Pat Nixon did well on the ice, too. Dick Nixon was a good sport but a bad skater and he spent most of his time hanging onto the railing. The young Nixons and their friends also played charades, went to the opera in Los Angeles, and occasionally splurged on spaghetti dinners. One of the high points of their early married life was a trip to Cuba for a short vacation.

Lacking in these years, as far as they were concerned, was any special interest in politics. Dick was a member of the local Republican party but he was not especially active. In the presidential election of 1940, he spoke warmly in favor of Wendell Wilkie, the Republican candidate for President, but that was the extent of his participation.

As far as the world situation was concerned, Richard Nixon had become increasingly worried in 1940 and 1941, in common with many other Americans. Europe and the Far East were threatened by the growing empires of Germany and Japan. Conflicts raged in Europe, Africa, Asia, and the South Pacific. American merchant ships were being attacked and sometimes sunk on the high seas. American war materials were being shipped to Britain and other countries whose defense and survival seemed vital to the United States. For the first time in America's history, her young men were drafted into military service in peace time. Most Americans, according to public opinion polls, were eager to avoid war if at all possible, but the overwhelming majority were also convinced that their country would become actively involved in it eventually.

For several years, President Franklin D. Roosevelt had been urging the nation to prepare for self-defense. A gleaming new flotilla, made up of aircraft carriers and other modern war vessels, had joined the older battleships of the Navy. It was hoped that, by remaining strong, the United States might discourage other nations from attacking its forces. But the Japanese, planning to knock the American Pacific Fleet out of commission in one blow, struck the naval base at Pearl Harbor, Hawaii, in a sneak attack on December 7,

1941. Nineteen ships were sunk or damaged and 2400 Americans lost their lives. The following day, the United States declared war on Japan and, a few days later, Germany and Italy declared war on the United States.

Angry Americans all across the continent demanded retaliation for the aggression committed by the Japanese. With the total mobilization of all resources, even comfortable, placid Whittier began to bustle with the activity of men departing for military service and industries changing over from peaceful to war-time production.

Pat and Dick Nixon were getting along fairly well on their joint salaries and were reaching the point where they felt they might be ready to put a down payment on a house. Yet it didn't seem right to them, somehow, for Dick to be safe and prospering on the home front while others were being trained to fight for their country in faraway places. At this point in his life, Richard Nixon faced one of his most serious decisions. As a Quaker, he held peace to be man's greatest glory; yet he valued his country's safety beyond estimation. Part of him longed to enlist in the armed forces and to volunteer for the most dangerous duty available; another part, backed by his family and many of his closest friends, urged him to uphold the peaceful ideal of the Friends to the fullest.

He compromised, for the sake of his family. With Pat's approval, he went to Washington, D.C., in January, 1942, to seek a civilian job where he might, somehow, help the war effort. At that time, government rationing was just beginning and there was real need for well-educated and hard-working civil servants to draw up and interpret regulations. Dick started work right away, at a salary of less than half what he had been earning as a lawyer.

He worked for the O.P.A., the Office of Price Administration, a newly created government bureau responsible for keeping control over prices and rents. This made him feel that he was doing something positive, however small, for the war effort. Incidentally, it gave him a worthwhile insight into government service. "I learned respect," he later said, "for the thousands of hard-working government employees and an equal contempt for most of the political appointees at the top. I saw government overlapping and government empire-building at first hand."

Although his work, dealing with tire rationing, was important, it was not very satisfying to him. Dick Nixon wanted a more active role in the war, preferably in the armed forces. He carefully hinted of his desires to his mother, laying the groundwork for her understanding of his decision. Hannah Nixon, quick to sense the needs of her children, understood and as she later said: "Though I'm a pacifist, I didn't try to stop him." So Richard Nixon enlisted in the United States Navy. Because he was a lawyer, he received a direct commission as a lieutenant, junior grade.

In September of 1942, he was assigned to Quonset, Rhode Island, for his initial training. At its completion, he put in a request for overseas duty but was sent instead to a naval air station in Ottumwa, Iowa. Although this was far from the sea duty he had hoped for, he felt it was an improvement over his duties with the O.P.A. At Ottumwa, he was an aide to a higher officer for some six months. It was a pleasant life and Dick was particularly happy to have Pat with him as a

"Navy wife." She had backed his decision to join the Navy and now set up a temporary home at Ottumwa. To keep busy while Dick was on duty, she took a position as a bank teller.

The six months spent in Ottumwa gave Dick Nixon the chance to study the Midwest closely. Few young Americans at that time could boast of being as widely traveled in the United States as he was at the age of thirty—he knew his native California well and his many lengthy debating tours had familiarized him with the Pacific Northwest and with the southwestern states. In addition, three years of living in North Carolina as a law student gave him some understanding of the American South. His months of naval air duty in Iowa helped him round out his geographical education. About the only areas he had not touched were the Middle Atlantic and the New England regions, except for brief visits. Perhaps Richard Nixon had inherited a little of the wanderlust that his father, Frank Nixon, had shown in his early life.

Richard Nixon's next move took him over six thousand miles across the Pacific Ocean. In the spring of 1943, he asked for overseas duty and was granted it. His orders took him first to San Francisco, to wait for transportation to the war zone. Pat set up living quarters in that California city and found a job as an economist with a West Coast office of the O.P.A., Dick's old government outfit.

After a long voyage by ship and airplane, Lieutenant Nixon reached the Pacific theater, where he was assigned to the South Pacific Combat Air Transport Command. During his fifteen months of combat duty, he served on Vella

Lavella, Guadalcanal, Bougainville, and Green Islands, all part of the Solomon Islands group in the South Pacific. He was not a flying officer. His duties were less spectacular than that, but were equally important. His chief job was to take a group of enlisted men to a newly opened air base and to make sure that the planes using it were supplied with bombs and fuel and other essentials.

Lieutenant Nixon was responsible for seeing that the enlisted men working under him performed their tasks satisfactorily. He took his duties very seriously. After planning an operation carefully, he did not always sit back and watch the men load and unload planes. He sometimes joined in the physical work himself when he felt he could help get it done faster in an emergency.

As an officer, Dick was responsible for the supervision and well-being of his "men," the enlisted men assigned to him. He came to know them well during the months they served together, as he proved when he described them individually in his letters to his family, telling of his experiences. As always, he was Nixon the teacher when he had an opportunity. He began an informal school and taught business law to anyone interested.

Naturally, he kept in close touch with Pat and the rest of the family back home. When his youngest brother Edward graduated from grammar school, he made a deal with him to keep him studying. For every hundred pages Edward read, his older brother promised to send him ten savings stamps. These stamps were sold by the government to raise money for the war effort. When enough of them were saved, they could be converted into a war bond.

Richard Nixon's attention to detail won him promotion to lieutenant, senior grade, as well as earning for him the respect of his fellow officers. He not only performed his duties well but he went beyond them, adding a Nixon touch to his job. By ceaseless scrounging, he set up a little stand where personnel passing through the base could get a hamburger, a sandwich, coffee, and other refreshments. This was provided free of charge and was a great morale booster. It was done without much fanfare. In fact, some of its patrons never knew who had organized it until years later.

With his fellow officers, "Nick," as he was often called, loosened up a bit. He began to smoke and to take a drink occasionally, and learned the art of playing poker. In military service, as he found out, there was either too much to do or too little, so he and his friends spent the idle hours playing cards. After taking lessons for a few days, Dick felt qualified to risk some of his pay at the card table. He became a good poker player and a steady winner, collecting quite a bit of money in his leisure time.

The war added a great deal to Dick Nixon's understanding of life. He saw much misery in the faces of wounded troops flown into his base in lumbering transport planes. He was in danger himself from enemy bombardment and once lived through twenty-eight days of bombing in a thirty-day period. He won two battle stars, yet when people asked him what it was like out there in the Pacific, he shrugged off their inquiry by saying that all he did in the South Pacific was to get a case of tropical fungus.

* * *

While Lieutenant Richard Nixon was serving in the South Pacific, another Navy lieutenant was stationed on other islands in the Solomons group. He was four years younger than Dick, but they both had a good deal in common. Both had played college football, both were of Irish descent, both were junior naval officers, both were idealistic young men, looking for ways to help the war effort. Dick had his own small supply command and a handful of enlisted men to help him. Lieutenant John Fitzgerald Kennedy was commander of a Patrol Torpedo Boat (the famous *P.T. 109*) with a small crew of Navy men under him. Lieutenant Kennedy had been tied to a desk job for months, just as Nixon had been in 1942. And, like Nixon, Kennedy left San Francisco in 1943 for combat duty. Kennedy got more than his share of it when *P.T. 109* was sunk by a Japanese destroyer in the summer of 1943. He heroically brought his crew through the ordeal, even though he was injured, and he won several medals for his bravery. But when a young boy asked him how he got to be a war hero, he answered: "They sank my boat."

In the summer of 1944, Lieutenant Richard Nixon was ordered back to the United States. He was assigned to a naval base near Alameda, California, as a transportation officer. Later, he was transferred to the East Coast, where he worked as a lawyer, helping to end war contracts which the Navy had with private companies. In this job, the Nixon approach to details paid off handsomely and he helped save the government several million dollars. He was given a naval citation for this service and was promoted to lieutenant commander in October, 1945.

This last phase of his naval duties took him to Baltimore, New York, and Philadelphia, where he served in various naval facilities. In downtown New York, he was assigned to an office in a skyscraper high above the street. From this vantage point, he was able to view one of the great moments in American history—the ticker tape parade which welcomed General Dwight D. Eisenhower home from the Allied victory in Europe. It was the first time that Nixon saw Eisenhower.

World War II, with its destruction and sacrifices and parades, had finally come to an end. It was time to return to ordinary life. Like millions of young men, Dick Nixon had lived in an atmosphere of intense idealistic activity for several years. The war over, there was a natural letdown. There would be new challenges, he knew, and the pleasures of family life and home living. But a certain period of readjustment was needed. As he waited for his discharge from the Navy at his assignment base in Baltimore, he had plenty of time to think and plan.

The goal that he and Pat had set for themselves was home ownership. Pat had lived on a family farm until she was seventeen, so knew the comforts of having a home of one's own, but all her adult life so far had been spent in rented apartments. During the war, she and Dick had continued to plan and save for their dream house. Between the two of them, the Nixons had put aside quite a bit of money toward their goal. Their first child was expected early in 1946, so things looked good for them. Yet, there was something missing for Dick as he contemplated his future while serving out his time in Baltimore. Returning to Whittier, practicing law, raising a family, owning a home—these were wonderful things to look forward to, but Dick Nixon was never completely satisfied unless he was doing something extra.

The invitation to do "something extra" came in November, 1945, in the form of a telegram from Whittier. It was an invitation to an election.

CHAPTER V

ᑯᗢᗝᑌ

In the early months of 1947, almost unnoticed by an America preoccupied with buying homes, raising families, getting educated, and trying to forget wartime memories, two young Navy veterans faced each other on a debate platform in the small Pennsylvania town of McKeesport. As they stepped to the podium, Congressman Richard M. Nixon and Congressman John F. Kennedy had every right to feel modestly proud of the small part they were playing in the management of their country through their membership in the House of Representatives of the Eightieth Congress of the United States.

They were on opposite sides of the political fence, Kennedy representing the Eleventh Congressional District of Massachusetts as a Democrat while Republican Nixon stood for the Twelfth of California. Their political differences did not prevent Kennedy and Nixon from becoming personal friends. On the other hand, their friendship did not prevent them from disagreeing with each other vigorously in public whenever their political beliefs clashed. The subject of their Pennsylvania debate was a brand new labor bill, the Taft-Hartley bill, which was then the center of great controversy.

The road to the House of Representatives had not been easy for either man. After his military service, John Kennedy took up a career in journalism briefly, but soon abandoned it in favor of politics. He decided to run for Congress from the same Congressional District in which his father, Joseph P. Kennedy, former United States Ambassador to Great Britain, had been born. Before he could get the Democratic party's nomination, however, he had to defeat nine other Democrats who also wanted the endorsement. He did this in a "primary election," that is, an election held to determine the candidate whom the party members preferred to run against the opposition party's candidate in the "general election."

While John Kennedy was seeking a Congressional seat in the Massachusetts delegation, Richard Nixon was doing the same thing in California, at the suggestion of a group of Republicans from the Twelfth Congressional District.

For ten years, Congressman Jerry Voorhis, a Democrat, had represented that district. He seemed to enjoy what politicians call a "safe" seat in Congress, that is, there didn't appear to be anyone who could beat him. In the summer of 1945, a meeting of leading Republicans was held to see if anything could be done to defeat Jerry Voorhis in the 1946 general election. As they discussed this problem, the situation seemed more and more hopeless. Voorhis was just too big a vote-getter to be challenged successfully. Nevertheless, they had to try.

To make sure that their search for a candidate was conducted over the widest possible range, the party leaders organized a large fact-finding committee consisting of persons from all walks of life. Wallace Newman, Richard Nixon's former football coach; Harry Schuyler, a prominent businessman and old Nixon family friend; and Herman Perry, manager of the Bank of America branch in Whittier, who had known Franklin Milhous, Dick's grandfather, were influential members of this group.

Herman Perry was convinced that the best candidate for the congressional nomination was Richard Nixon and, after interviewing a number of able but not completely acceptable prospective choices, many other Republicans began to feel the same way. It was Perry who sent the telegram from Whittier to Richard Nixon while he was still a Navy officer in Baltimore. Years later, Richard Nixon said that, if it had not been for Herman Perry, it "is very unlikely that I would be holding a political office today."

In answer to the telegram, Dick Nixon telephoned Mr. Perry and agreed to fly home from Baltimore to discuss the matter. He obtained a short leave and, in early November, 1945, flew to Whittier to meet the committee. Over seventy fact-finders listened while he explained his political philosophy.

In crisp, businesslike tones, Richard Nixon declared that he did not believe in government handouts for returning veterans. He said that he, along with most G.I.'s, wanted jobs and the chance to start their own businesses, instead of government programs or government control. He answered all questions directly, revealing his belief in moderate Republican ideas. The fact-finding committee was so impressed with him that more than fifty of them voted to recommend him to be the Republican party's candidate for the United States Congress.

Now the work began. When the congratulations and handshaking were over, Pat and Dick Nixon began to look at what they had gotten themselves into. He was still in the Navy, they were expecting a baby in a couple of months, and they had their little nest egg in the bank for buying a house. In January, 1946, Richard Nixon left the Navy and returned home; then he and Pat plunged into the campaign with all their energy.

There were many difficulties and obstacles to overcome, but this made the challenge all the more absorbing. They rented a small office in an old building in Whittier, borrowed a typewriter, a sofa, and some office furniture from friends and relatives, and enlisted the aid of a few volunteers. The "volunteer" who gave the most help was Hannah Nixon. Aside from her moral support, Mrs. Nixon was on hand when Pat and Dick's first child, a girl, was born in February, 1946. She was named Patricia, for her mother, although she would later be called "Tricia." Pat Nixon gave the baby her undivided attention for a few weeks, then rejoined Dick on the campaign trail, leaving Tricia in Hannah Nixon's competent hands. Thereafter, the latter became an important part of her son's political career. Whenever he ran for public office or whenever he took his wife with him on trips, Grandmother Nixon was always there to watch over Tricia and, after 1948, their second daughter, Julie.

During this first compaign, the Nixons found another valuable political ally and a good friend as well in a Californian named Murray Chotiner. A professional campaign manager who had helped other West Coast candidates organize successful political campaigns, he was assigned to the Nixon camp by Republican leaders, to offer a little advice. Murray Chotiner had a few simple rules to guide candidates —find out what your best talents are and use these to the fullest; find out your opponent's weakest points and hammer away at them; don't attack the opposition *party*, only the opposition *candidate*.

In planning Richard Nixon's campaign for Congressman, Chotiner suggested that his candidate use his public-speaking talents whenever possible. This advice led Dick Nixon to address veterans' groups, labor organizations, and business clubs. He also went directly to the people, meeting them on the streets on handshaking tours. This last activity he found to be one of the hardest chores in political life, since he had always been somewhat shy and reserved, not one to strike up conversations with strangers easily. Nevertheless, he proved to be as convincing on a person-to-person basis as he was on the speaker's platform, so Murray Chotiner urged him to get out and meet the people as much as possible.

After the first enthusiastic response from friends and relatives, the "Nixon for Congress" campaign lagged. Nobody seemed to care very much about whether Voorhis or Nixon sat for the Twelfth "C.D." of California. Richard Nixon was almost unknown outside of his own home town, and Whittier was only a small part of the district. The campaign office ran out of stamps, while printing bills, telephone expenses, and other costs continued to grow, with very little money trickling in as campaign contributions. Pat and Dick

Nixon watched their small store of savings begin to dwindle. Nothing seemed to go right. One day when Pat was in the office, people began coming in, asking for her husband's campaign leaflets. She handed them out in large batches until there were practically none left. Only later did she realize that the literature had been taken to be thrown away.

Despite the fact that Richard Nixon hit hard at the weaknesses of his opponent, few people showed much interest in his efforts. When the primary election was held, things became even worse. California primaries in those days were not limited just to party members. Under a "cross-filing" law, Nixon and Voorhis filed for both the Democratic and Republican primaries in their district. Voorhis won the Democratic primary and Nixon took the Republican one, but Voorhis received many Republican votes and wound up topping Nixon by thousands of votes in the total count of both parties.

That was it! Richard Nixon just couldn't win, said many political leaders, and the Republicans were only wasting time and money supporting him. It would be better to expend their efforts and funds on other Republican candidates throughout the state.

But while things looked bleak, the Nixon team's backers were not yet ready to give up. The idea occurred to them that their man had not been using his talents to the fullest, according to Murray Chotiner's first law for candidates. Nixon was a champion debater, it was pointed out, so why not use this talent? But some advisers said to forget the idea, since Jerry Voorhis was an excellent debater himself and had won his first election to Congress after debating his opponent. After a good deal of consideration, the Nixon team decided to send a challenge off to Voorhis' headquarters. It was accepted, and a series of debates was scheduled. Almost at once, interest in the campaign picked up.

Americans love a contest—quiz show, football game, horse race, it doesn't matter what the contestants are doing. The people love the battle for its own sake. Crowds flocked to the meeting halls to hear the five Voorhis-Nixon debates, the attendance at one of these reaching an estimated five thousand. People were now talking about the issues and the candidates.

Dick Nixon had studied Congressman Voorhis' weakest points and stressed these. He claimed that Voorhis had not done enough for his district, that he had become so isolated in Washington that he had lost touch with the people of his community. He also attacked Voorhis' voting record, which did not reflect the wishes of the majority of voters in the Twelfth C.D., according to the Nixon assessment.

Whatever the reason or reasons may have been—the debates, or the differences in ideas, or Dick Nixon's youth and personality—the challenger swamped Congressman Voorhis at the polls in November, 1946. The vote was 65,000 to 50,000, a clear sweep for the apprentice candidate. What is more, those who voted for Nixon included many Democrats who, for their own reasons, chose him over Voorhis.

Jerry Voorhis was a fine man, and a good sport. He sent the winner his congratulations and suggested that the two get together to discuss the problems of the district. Nothing happened for some time, until one day, when Voorhis was returning to his office from lunch, he found Congressman-elect Richard Nixon waiting for him. They talked for about an hour about their mutual responsibilities and parted as friends.

Dick Nixon had finally achieved the "something extra" he had dreamed of during the last days of his career as a naval officer. He now had a new and challenging vocation which stemmed directly from his training and experience as a lawyer—he was a politician. To many people, the word politician has undesirable meanings. They think of an insincere person, an apple-polisher, a shady dealer, whenever the term is used. To Richard Nixon, "the function of a politician is to make a free society work." This is a simple definition, but the simplest goals are often the hardest to achieve.

When Richard Nixon arrived in Washington, he found out that becoming a Congressman was a lot like starting any other job. The first order of business was to set up a home for his family in their new location. In the suburbs of Virginia, miles from Washington, he and Pat found an apartment they could rent for eighty dollars a month. They did not possess a great deal of wealth. They had their depleted savings, a 1946 car, some furniture, and Dick's life insurance. But an abundance of money had never meant much to the Nixons. Pat was a good manager. She served as wife, mother, cook, laundress, and home decorator for the family, as well as being an invaluable campaign manager, with the help of Grandmother Nixon.

While Pat set up things at home, Congressman Nixon reported to the Capitol in January, 1947, to assume his new post in the House of Representatives. He was extremely fortunate from the start in that, although the President,

Harry S. Truman, was a Democrat, the Republicans were in control of Congress. This put them in a position to push bright newcomers like Nixon into the public eye. But even with this advantage, the status of a freshman in the Congress is like that of a freshman in high school or any other place. Along with all the other new arrivals, Richard Nixon received the worst office facilities, the fewest helpers, the least interesting committee assignments, and the hardest extra chores, with little voice in the actual running of things. All the big decisions were made by the long-term members of the House. The young fellows were expected to follow the rule: "To get along, go along."

This was disillusioning to eager Congressman Nixon, as he later admitted. He had come to Washington filled with great ideas for reforming the country and he wound up snowed under by paper work and what seemed to be unimportant routine matters. He was luckier than most young congressmen, though. He was given posts on the Education and Labor Committee and on the Un-American Activities Committee.

Richard Nixon was obliged to gear himself to the way things were done in Congress. Over the years of its existence, Congress has evolved methods of doing things which are slow but which have proved to be effective. One method used is the committee system, in which the major concerns of Congress are divided into such committees as Public Works, Armed Services, Foreign Affairs, etc. Some committees have dozens of members, while others have only a handful. In addition, there are subcommittees of the standing (or permanent) committees. Dick Nixon was new to all this but he buckled down to learn the system, just as he had done in college, law school, the Navy, and while campaigning for a political office.

He soon acquired a reputation for being a hard-working, perceptive, and humane legislator. He listened, soaking up whatever he could learn from any source. Since the younger members of the House are apt to be ignored, Dick Nixon and a few other newcomers organized the "Chowder and Marching Society," a group of fifteen novice Republican Congressmen who stuck together so that their voices might be better heard by the older leadership. They met on Wednesdays to exchange views and experiences.

In his first term as a Congressman, Richard Nixon encountered a force he had long heard of but had not yet confronted face to face—international communism. It would begin to play a large part in his life, as it had and would in the lives of millions of people the world over.

Communism is a basic belief, similar to a religious faith. It was founded upon the teachings of Karl Marx, who lived during the nineteenth century. It has a large body of doctrines, just as religious faiths do, and it has its missionaries, hymns, "martyrs," and even "church" elders. Yet, although it resembles a religion, communism, or Marxism, as it is sometimes called, actually denies the existence of God. It is a kind of rival religion to Christianity, Judaism, and the other faiths based on the worship of a Creator.

For years, communists were weak in numbers and scattered all over the world, but in 1917, a group of determined revolutionaries took advantage of Russia's defeat in World War I to seize control of the government. After years of bloody warfare, a communist dictator named Lenin gained absolute control over the Russian people and began to impose his idea of communism upon them. When Lenin died, he was replaced by Joseph Stalin, who had his own idea of what communism should be.

There were then really two kinds of communism in existence: the dream and the real thing. In theory, communism offered a golden dream, based on a belief in social justice, economic equality, and political liberty. Many people in Russia and outside of it accepted this dream and sacrificed greatly for it. When applied to real conditions in Russia, however, communism turned out to be a force which promoted just as much injustice and inequality as the old government in Russia had. Still, many intelligent persons, including Americans, believed in the dream of communism and thought Russia was the living example of it.

The goal of Stalin was to achieve Russian domination of Europe and Asia. By the time Congressman Nixon reached Washington, Russian controlled or influenced governments had been set up in East Germany, Poland, Bulgaria, Albania, Yugoslavia, and North Korea. During his first term, Hungary and Rumania became Russian puppets, and communists were hard at work trying to undermine the governments of Greece, Turkey, and China.

Practically everything in which Richard Nixon was directly or indirectly involved during the first four years of his career as a national legislator was touched by some aspect of communism. For example, in his first term as a Congressman, he was picked to serve on a special committee which journeyed to the war-torn sections of Europe in order to

learn what was needed to help them recover. Only by giving some kind of aid to Europe, many Americans thought,
could the nations of Italy, Greece, Turkey, France, West
Germany, and other free countries be kept from falling
under the domination of Russia as the Eastern European
countries had.

This special committee, under the leadership of Representative Christian Herter of Massachusetts, spent about a
month touring the Continent. By the time the members returned home, they had received a broad education in human
misery. Dick Nixon had talked to English politicians, had
discovered the views of Italian peasants and Greek soldiers,
and had built up a store of ideas and facts which went into
the vast report the Herter committee prepared, showing
what was needed to restore Europe to normal economic life
and to prevent the still-independent countries from becoming part of Russia's communist empire.

Out of these findings came the plan for American aid to
the war-ravaged nations of Europe known as the Marshall
Plan. This program was named after General George C.
Marshall, one of America's best known soldier-statesmen.

As a member of the Herter committee and of the House
of Representatives, Richard Nixon had a small share in the
development of this plan. During the next few years, he
supported policies designed to help other nations to stave off
communism, gave his vote to laws strengthening the armed
forces of the United States, and urged the nation to keep on
taking an active part in world leadership. He also advised
his countrymen to teach all school children about com-

munism, its goals and beliefs, so that they might be able to cope with its designs better when they grew up.

Many Americans at this time were worried about overseas communism but could not see it as a danger at home. Actually, some Americans who were sympathetic to communism became agents of the Russian government during World War II. They secured jobs in such vital areas as government, labor unions, schools, and the film industry. Others, who were not outright spies, were also recruited. Most of these were well-meaning Americans who failed to see that Stalin was using the dreams of communism to hide the real goal of Russian expansion.

Richard Nixon was aware that communism existed in his country, too, but it was not until an August morning in 1948 that he saw just how much of a menace it was. As a member of the House Un-American Activities Committee, he listened to witnesses testifying about the internal dangers threatening the United States. The particular witness he heard that hot summer morning was an ex-communist named Whittaker Chambers, an editor of *Time* magazine.

Chambers, a rumpled, rather unimpressive looking man, confessed to having been a communist courier, part of a network of foreign and American agents spying on behalf of Russia. He received stolen documents from American government officials and passed these on to Russian agents. After doing this for years, he repudiated his communistic beliefs and stopped his espionage activity. In an effort to repair some of the damage he had caused, he turned on his former fellow-conspirators and named them as his accomplices. One of these was a high-ranking State Department official named Alger Hiss, who had been one of President Roosevelt's advisers at the Yalta Conference in 1945. Later, after his testimony before the Committee, Whittaker Chambers repeated his charge over the widely viewed television program "Meet the Press." Chambers said: "Alger Hiss was a communist and may still be one."

Alger Hiss was a neat, handsome, and prominent man, who included Presidents, Supreme Court justices, and cabinet officers among his acquaintances. He denied ever knowing a person named Chambers and, when Chambers persisted in his accusations, sued him for $75,000.

Both men were called to testify before the House Un-American Activities Committee, so Richard Nixon had the opportunity to compare them at close range. By this time, he had met a great many men of all types and had learned to read them pretty well. Something in the tone and manner of Chambers told him that this man was speaking the truth, and something equally sure was telling him that Hiss was not. When asked if he knew Chambers, for example, Hiss replied that he had never known a man *by the name* of Chambers. Nixon was puzzled by this statement. Why hadn't Hiss stated flatly that he had never known Whittaker Chambers? This and other weak testimony raised doubts about Hiss in Richard Nixon's legal mind.

Still, when the Committee, the Congress, and the public appraised both men, Hiss seemed the more believable. He was always smooth, even, and cool, while Chambers seemed uncertain and edgy. Newspapers began to say that the House Un-American Activities Committee was acting irresponsibly in taking Chambers so seriously. Even President Truman agreed with the idea that the whole investigation was a false trail.

When other members of the committee were in favor of dropping the whole Hiss-Chambers matter, Richard Nixon argued against it. Then the pressure on him began. Members of Congress, newspaper people, and powerful political allies of Hiss began to hint that Nixon was only trying to make a big name for himself by standing alone against the President and many other persons in and out of government. Nixon argued so well against dropping the matter that he was appointed to head a sub-committee to carry on the investigation. Hiss either knew Chambers or he did not. One or the other man had to be lying. Dick Nixon waded wholeheartedly into the biggest assignment of his life so far. This was a tough position in which the young Congressman found himself. Later, he called it the first of six crises he faced between 1948 and 1960.

Step by step, detail by detail, the sub-committee and its investigators carefully drew evidence from Hiss and Chambers. Hiss finally admitted that he had known Chambers, but not by his real name. One by one, the facts came out, Chambers offering powerful proof of his testimony in the form of documents stolen from the Department of State which Hiss had given him. These papers, which Chambers had hidden in a hollow pumpkin on his farm for a short time, became famous the world over as the "Pumpkin Papers."

Day after day, the case crowded out other items of the news. Nixon's name and photograph were before the American people in newspapers and magazines all across the country. A great deal of what was written was uncomplimentary. Congressman Nixon learned on a wide scale that you can never take a strong position in public life without making enemies as well as friends.

Alger Hiss was finally convicted of perjury, or lying under oath. He spent over three years in federal prison. The Hiss case made Richard Nixon a national and international figure, and it had a most important influence on his life. He later wrote that some people had told him he would have been elected President of the United States in 1960 if it had not been for the Hiss case, because he made so many enemies at that time. But, he added, other people reminded him that he might never have been nominated as Vice-Presidential running mate to General Dwight D. Eisenhower if it had not been for the fame he gained by his part in the Hiss-Chambers affair.

Ordinarily, just learning the fundamentals of being a legislator would occupy a new congressman's full energies. This, plus his involvement in the Hiss case, kept Richard Nixon going eighteen hours a day. He did not have much time to enjoy the company of Pat and his daughters, Tricia and baby Julie. When he could get away from work for a short time, he and Pat went bicycling or picnicking. He also found a good deal of comfort in the fact that his parents had moved to a farm in nearby Pennsylvania. When he needed time to reflect on a problem, as during the Hiss case, he would make a quick trip to the farm and spend a short time there in solitude. Hannah Nixon provided her invaluable services as a baby sitter to allow Dick and Pat to take brief vacations and to campaign for reelection.

In the California Congressional elections of 1948, Richard Nixon had had little difficulty in winning both the Democratic and Republican primaries, then going on to win the contest for Congressman in the general election in November over his Democratic opponent, Steve Zetterberg. Two years later, in 1950, he faced another important decision—whether to run for the Senate or to stay on as a member of the House of Representatives. The Senate had great advantages. The term of office there was six years; that of a House member was only two. While there were 435 members of the House, the Senate had 96. Dick and Pat decided that he should risk everything on a campaign to represent the State of California in the Senate.

These were days of increased tension for the United States. Determined to add to his victories in bringing communism to Eastern Europe, Premier Stalin had stepped up aid to communists in China, helping them to overthrow the government in that country. By the end of 1949, communism was victorious in China and the free Chinese government fled to the island of Formosa or Taiwan.

Not content with this triumph, Stalin aided the communist government of North Korea in an invasion of free South Korea in June, 1950. President Truman reacted strongly to this threat and sent United States troops to defend South Korea. Soon, about a dozen free world nations were fighting alongside the American and South Korean defenders. Within a few months, the North Korean army was in retreat and the government was crumbling. At this point, however, communist China intervened and the free world nations were then faced with a powerful military machine equipped with enormous manpower.

In this distracted atmosphere, the elections of 1950 were held. Richard Nixon's opponent for the Senate was a Congresswoman named Helen G. Douglas, who had a strong record of service to the country in the House of Representatives. Mrs. Douglas campaigned hard and tirelessly and both sides exchanged bitter charges over unfair campaign tactics, as is often the case in hard-fought political contests.

For Pat and Dick Nixon, this became the fight of their lives. Instead of being confined to a fairly small district, as is the case with a race for Congress, a senatorial campaign takes in every corner of a state. California was the second largest state in both area (after Texas) and population (after New York) at the time, and candidates were expected to meet as many voters as they could. Borrowing a station wagon to serve as campaign headquarters on wheels, the Nixons motored from town to town, meeting people, answering questions, and passing out leaflets. Sometimes Dick spoke to a handful of voters; other times it seemed as if he were shaking hands with all 10½ million inhabitants of California on the same day. His hand would be swollen, his feet burning, and still people came. Sometimes "wise guys" made unpleasant remarks; other times, older citizens would express their thanks to him for the job he was doing for the country. It was a bruising, exhausting fight, but Dick Nixon carried off the prize by a majority of 680,000 votes. His victory made him the youngest member of that session of the United States Senate. He was thirty-seven at the time of his election, while the average age of a senator was over fifty.

One of the special rewards of participating in a campaign such as the one he had just completed was the opportunity it gave Richard Nixon to meet outstanding people about whom he had read for years. Herbert Hoover, former President of the United States, became a friend and introduced him to many notables, including General Dwight Eisenhower. This was the second time Dick Nixon had seen the General, the first time being when he had spied Ike from his office window high above the victory parade in New York City.

During his years in the House and the Senate, Richard Nixon was involved in most of the important issues of the time. On his own, he sponsored nearly fifty bills and he was co-sponsor with other lawmakers more than two dozen times. He introduced a bill to strengthen the United Nations, urged the admission of Hawaii and Alaska as states, supported a movement to give the District of Columbia more freedom from Congressional control, proposed international disarmament under reasonable supervision, and suggested many other reforms. Not all of these passed the House and Senate, of course, but Richard Nixon managed to earn a good batting average, considering his newness in office.

One of his most important duties in Congress was to serve on the House Education and Labor Committee, where he helped to write the Taft-Hartley labor act. The purpose of this Republican-sponsored measure was to curb the abuses which some labor leaders were charged with and to protect the laborer, the labor union, and the country from the excessive use of power by a few irresponsible men. Some Congressmen, including Representative John F. Kennedy, thought the measure would harm labor. It was this measure that Congressman Nixon had defended against the attacks of Congressman Kennedy in their debate at McKeesport, Pennsylvania, in 1947.

To the leaders of their parties, Nixon and Kennedy were men of the future. Richard Nixon's election to the Senate in 1950, on top of the fame he had won in the investigation of Alger Hiss, made him an important national figure. He had a good many friends in the "upper house," as the Senate is called, including Henry Cabot Lodge, Jr., from Massachusetts. Senator Lodge, whose family was one of the oldest and most distinguished in America, was a powerful leader in the Republican party. He was hoping that his party could induce General Eisenhower to run for the Presidency in 1952.

For Senator Nixon, the future looked good, with a full six years to serve in the United States Senate. He became a popular guest speaker at dinners and other gatherings. He met thousands of people, and was widely quoted in the newspapers. His willingness to take a stand on issues in which he believed made people listen to him and usually see things in pro-Nixon or anti-Nixon terms—no in between.

Pat Nixon was pleased with her husband's position as a Senator, not only because of her pride in him but also because she would not have to go through the rigors of campaigning every two years, as she had in 1946, 1948, and 1950. She was wrong there, however. The Nixons would do a bit of campaigning only two years after he ran for Senator.

CHAPTER VI

⸎

EVERY FOUR YEARS, the American people go through the process of electing a President. The election takes place in leap year, and during most of American history it has been held in November. A Presidential election year is often a tumultuous period, and stories of wild demonstrations, wild accusations, and even wilder promises fill the pages of the newspapers. Within the political parties, prospective candidates struggle for the nomination, and the winners go on to the contest between the parties.

Strange things happen during Presidential election years. Potential nominees who are well known suddenly give up and decide not to run, while little-known persons gain fame overnight. It is a year of surprises, and the year 1952 was no exception.

When Harry Truman announced, early in the year, that he would not be a candidate for the Presidency again, there was a frantic struggle to see which Democratic hopeful could gain the nomination. At the Democratic National Convention at Chicago in July, 1952, the Party chose Governor Adlai E. Stevenson of Illinois. As the Vice-Presidential candidate, the Democrats selected Senator John J. Sparkman of Alabama.

The Republican National Convention was also held in Chicago in July, although not during the same days. Senator Richard Nixon was one of the leaders of the California delegation, along with Governor Earl Warren and other well-known politicians. Although an ambitious man, it is doubtful that Richard Nixon had any hopes that he would play a vital part at the Convention. He and Pat went about their business, going to conferences, meeting other delegates and their wives, answering mail, and taking phone calls.

The real business of the Convention was to choose a popular and capable candidate. After a brief struggle, the party settled on Dwight D. Eisenhower. General Eisenhower had been President of Columbia University in New York City after the Second World War and had also served as commander of the forces of the North Atlantic Treaty Organization (NATO). This was an alliance between the United States and most of the non-communist nations of Europe. It was designed to protect all members from Russian aggression.

To Richard Nixon, Dwight Eisenhower was a perfect choice. Although not a professional politician, the General knew something about politics and a great deal about handling men. While commander of the Allied forces during World War II, he showed great skill as a diplomat, administrator, and decision-maker. Senator Nixon held many beliefs in common with "Ike," as he had discovered in 1951 while visiting the General at NATO headquarters in Paris.

After the selection of the Presidential candidate, the

choice of a Vice-Presidential running mate was the next order of business. This decision is usually left up to the Presidential candidate, since, if he becomes President, he will want a Vice President who is loyal, sympathetic to his views, and a capable successor in the event of his death. With great thoroughness, Dwight Eisenhower began to gather as much information and advice about potential running mates as possible. He and his advisers compiled a list of potential choices and Richard Nixon's name was on it.

When he read the press reports speculating on his possible candidacy, Senator Nixon bought extra copies of the newspapers to save for his children and grandchildren, because that was about as close as he ever expected to get to the Vice Presidency.

As the Convention was winding down, Dick Nixon was resting in his hotel room when he was interrupted by a call from Eisenhower headquarters, informing him that he had been selected as Ike's running mate. The Senator was thunderstruck! Pat was equally surprised when she heard the news on a television set in a nearby restaurant, where she was having a sandwich with friends. "We practically ran back to the hall," she wrote later on.

Just why did Eisenhower choose Nixon? There were many reasons. Not only was the young Senator well liked by his fellow Republicans, but he was also well known across the country and well thought of by many of his fellow citizens. He had also proved that he was not a man to follow extremes but believed in moderation, as Eisenhower did. He came from a large and populous state, which would be an advantage in the campaign. Finally, his youth would appeal to veterans and younger citizens. All of these reasons influenced his selection as running mate in 1952.

But would Richard Nixon agree to run for this position? He wondered if he could be as useful and active in the Vice Presidency as he was now in the Senate. Some people believed that the Vice Presidency was a very unimportant job. They compared it to the spare tire in a car—you never want to use it, but it's nice to have it on hand if you need it. Richard Nixon had no intention of being a spare tire.

Ike promised that the Vice President in his administration would have a busy and vital schedule and would become an important member of his "team." Swayed by this promise, Richard Nixon accepted the Vice-Presidential nomination. He never regretted jumping on the Eisenhower "bandwagon," and, as he came to know his running mate better, the younger man grew to like him more and more. As far as Ike was concerned, he later wrote of Dick Nixon that he "found him vigorous, alert, and intelligent," and was pleased to discover how "remarkably close together in political views generally" they were.

In addition to their political policies, they had a great deal in common personally. Both were small town boys. Ike's father had run a grocery store and had been a locomotive engineer. Dick's father had run a grocery store and had been a trolley-car motorman. Both candidates had grown up in very religious homes, Dick as a Quaker while Ike's family belonged to the Brethren of Christ. Both men had a good understanding of and hatred for communism and knew how to stand up to it; both were devoted to and proud of the American way of life. Both Eisenhower and

Nixon came from west of the Mississippi. Ike would be the first Texas-born person to become President and Dick the first Californian to win the Vice Presidency.

The 1952 campaign had its share of triumphs and setbacks for the Nixons. Soon after his nomination, Dick returned with Pat to Whittier, where a huge "homecoming" ceremony was held in his honor. Some twenty thousand persons turned out for the festivities at the Whittier College football field. It gave Richard Nixon a wonderful feeling to see his proud parents, his two brothers, relatives, teachers, friends, and supporters rallying to him in such a whole-hearted way. He might not have been a football star on this same field, but he was now in a struggle which demanded all the stamina and perseverance he had shown while on the team some twenty years earlier.

A few weeks later, the pleasant memories of the homecoming and other enjoyable ceremonies were forgotten when influential newspapers began to charge that, while he was a senator, Richard Nixon had been receiving money from a secret fund set up by wealthy men. The newspaper stories implied that the money was given to influence Dick Nixon to look out for the interests of the contributors. Soon, the news of the "secret Nixon fund" was circulating around the country. The victim of the stories was bewildered by them at first. He did have a carefully regulated and supervised political expense account amounting to over eighteen thousand dollars. This had been raised by donations from dozens of persons, including friends such as Dr. Paul Smith, his former teacher at Whittier. No one had been allowed to contribute too large an amount in order to avoid the possibility of anyone's trying to use the donation for selfish purposes. The fund provided Senator Nixon with the means of traveling between Washington and California, in order to help him keep in touch with the people of his state. It was also used for stationery, postage, and advertising expenses. Richard Nixon had not profited from the fund personally, although hostile newspaper critics hinted that he might have.

At the time the story broke, Dick Nixon was campaigning by train in California, traveling from town to town to meet and speak with the people and urge them to support the Eisenhower-Nixon ticket. Harsh accusations began to fly and vicious signs appeared. Perhaps the worst was directed toward Mrs. Nixon. It read: "Pat, what are you going to do with the bribe money?"

Richard Nixon could not believe what was happening. He knew that every person in public life, even extremely wealthy politicians, received political contributions from supporters. He realized that he was being smeared by the opposition, but what hurt him most was the word that several Republican newspapers were planning to urge Ike to drop him from the ticket. By now, he was indignant and angry. As his campaign train headed into Oregon, each stop became a duel with hecklers, some of whom tried to shout down his speeches. He decided that the best way to meet the attack was by going on television to tell his story.

At this point, all his years of speaking in public without a prepared speech came to his aid. On a plane flying from Oregon to the TV studio in Los Angeles, he outlined his thoughts on the backs of postcards until he had a general idea of what he was going to say. When he stepped before the cameras, his thoughts were clear in his mind, and the words which gave them life came spontaneously across the more than eight hundred TV and radio stations which carried the message. Only Pat and a few close associates were with him in the studio.

Dick Nixon described the fund completely, where it came from, and for what it was used. Then he went on to reveal his complete financial history, including his debts and other personal monetary details. He defended himself vigorously, and just as vigorously challenged the Democratic candidates to describe their personal finances in the same way. He also mentioned that Governor Stevenson had several funds built up by private contributions to assist Illinois state officials in carrying out their duties. These should be explained to the American people, Nixon suggested. And he added a very human family note—that his daughters had received a gift of a black-and-white cocker spaniel from a supporter in Texas. This dog, which his daughter Tricia had named Checkers, he was going to keep, he said, and he just wanted everyone to know that he was sure his enemies would start attacking him for this, too. Ever since, this broadcast has been called the "Checkers Speech."

In his conclusion, Richard Nixon stated that he was going to leave the decision over whether he should stay on the ticket or not to the leaders of the Republican party. But he urged any viewers who felt strongly about it to let these leaders know what they thought.

The cameras stopped and Dick Nixon realized that he had not told his audience where to write or telephone. He was also convinced that he had not "gone over," that he had not reached the public with his ideas. Pat assured him that the speech had been a great success and, by the time they had returned to their hotel, her judgment was proved to be correct. They were fairly mobbed by well-wishers and supporters.

Never had there been anything like that speech before in American political history. It had been viewed by some sixty million persons—the largest audience in television history previous to the 1960 election campaign. Telegrams, letters, and telephone calls flowed in from every corner of the nation. Since Dick Nixon had given no central address in his appeal for audience reaction, respondents sent their messages to him, to Eisenhower Headquarters, to Republican National Convention Headquarters in Washington, and to various other destinations. Over two million people answered his plea, and the answer they gave was to urge him to stay with the fight. Accompanying much of the mail were donations amounting to tens of thousands of dollars, more than enough to pay for the broadcast.

That night, addressing a political rally, Ike said: "I have seen brave men in tough situations. I have never seen anyone come through in better fashion than Senator Nixon did tonight." A few days later, Richard Nixon flew to West Virginia to discuss the matter further with Mr. Eisenhower, who declared that he was satisfied that his running mate had done nothing wrong. The affair, in fact, worked to the advantage of the Eisenhower-Nixon ticket. Senator Nixon's appearances drew larger crowds than before because of the interest which his broadcast had created.

In this crisis of his life, Dick Nixon had many friends, but none so strong and effective as his mother and father. Although no longer as active as they had been, they were still keen observers and gave wise advice. At the height of the funds crisis, Hannah Nixon, who was in Washington minding the children, sent her son the message: "Have faith, Mother." She also sent a longer telegram to General Eisenhower, assuring him that he could have "implicit faith" in Richard's "integrity and honesty." Frank Nixon reacted to the whole thing in his salty way by saying, "It looks to me as if the Democrats have given themselves a good kick in the seat of the pants."

The Checkers Speech, like the Hiss-Chambers affair before it, had taxed all of Richard Nixon's stamina and courage because he knew how much was at stake. It left him with millions of friends, but, not surprisingly, with many enemies, some of whom would do anything to drag him down. There were powerful enemies in the newspaper field, and while most of these were at least fair to him, some would accept any story no matter how farfetched it seemed, as long as it showed Richard Nixon in a bad light. During his career in politics, Nixon once wrote, he had been accused of "bigamy, forgery, drunkenness, insanity, thievery," and many other unpleasant activities. This was a difficult price to pay for staying in the political arena.

The campaign between the Eisenhower-Nixon and Stevenson-Sparkman teams wound up on November 4, 1952, with a resounding victory for the Republican candidates. Eisenhower received almost thirty-four million votes to twenty-seven million for Stevenson. In January of 1953, the new administration began to function under a Republican President and Congress for the first time in over twenty years.

One of the drawbacks about this victory was the slim, one-vote margin by which the Republicans held control of the Senate (forty-eight to forty-seven, with one independent Senator). This narrow edge gave Vice President Nixon a place in American history which few "Veeps" have held, because it was one of his duties to cast a vote in the event of a tie. During the course of his Vice Presidency, he cast eight tie-breaking votes, more than any other man in history.

The main duty of the Vice President, according to the Constitution of the United States, is to serve as presiding officer of the Senate. This brought Richard Nixon back to his associates of the year before, now with the official title "President of the Senate." In this position, Mr. Nixon was able to give interpretations to rules of the Senate in order to make business flow faster.

Actually, although the Senate stays in session for months, the Vice President does not spend long hours simply sitting in front of it to keep order. This would be a great waste of time, as both Republicans and Democrats have recognized. Only about 5 or 10 per cent of a Vice President's time is spent presiding over the Senate. The rest of the time, he attends meetings, heads committees, does endless paper work, and studies domestic and foreign events to keep posted on all the latest turns in world affairs. Out of a fourteen-hour day, Mr. Nixon once estimated, he might spend half an hour in the Senate.

During his two terms as Vice President, he attended over

five hundred top-level meetings of the government and was the chairman of nearly fifty of these. This, of course, did not include meetings with the President, Cabinet officers, and other high-ranking figures, alone or in small groups. This placed him at the decision-making center of the nation and, while President Eisenhower made the decisions in his own administrations, he always called for the opinion of his closest advisers, including his Vice President.

The President kept his word to Richard Nixon—he gave him plenty of work to do. One of these duties included working with Senators and Representatives to secure their support for Eisenhower-backed legislation. Since he had been a senator himself, Dick Nixon knew well the problems and working methods of lawmaking. This made it easier for him to influence such legislation as the Civil Rights Acts of 1957 and 1960 which gave protection to persons who had the right to vote but were denied it because of their race or color.

Knowing how strongly he felt about discrimination, particularly against Black persons and other minorities, the President appointed Richard Nixon to head a government committee to secure equal treatment for all Americans. The committee worked directly with those firms doing business with the government. It was credited with urging the elimination of discrimination in hundreds of cases and was widely praised by persons of both political parties and of different religious and ethnic groups.

During the years from 1953 to 1961, Richard Nixon met many challenges. One of these came in 1955, when President Eisenhower had a serious heart attack. This was a great shock to the country but it was an even greater one for the Vice President since, in addition to the personal sorrow he felt over his stricken friend and leader, he was forced to contemplate the prospect of his own succession to the Presidency in the event of Dwight Eisenhower's death. It was an awesome thing to consider. Fortunately, the President recovered and was able to resume his duties.

During the crisis of his illness and the period of his convalescence, the President called on Richard Nixon to meet with Cabinet and other officers in order to help handle the usual business of government. Dwight Eisenhower had created a well-trained "team" of top advisers, so things operated smoothly and successfully while he was ill.

A few years later, Ike had another attack of illness which left him with some slight speech difficulties. This raised an extremely important question. Suppose, in the future, a President of the United States was struck with a sickness which left him alive but mentally or physically unable to carry on his work? There was nothing in the Constitution to cover this problem, so, when Ike recovered, he entered into an agreement with Richard Nixon which allowed the Vice President to *act as* (but not *be*) President in the event of such an illness. Later Presidents and their Vice Presidents adopted similar agreements until Congress passed and the states ratified the Twenty-fifth Amendment to the Constitution (1967) which provided for the orderly succession of the Vice President temporarily under closely regulated conditions.

Vice President Nixon's responsibilities under President Eisenhower kept him busy in every sphere. Since Dick

Nixon was known as a professional politician, he was called upon to help elect Republicans to Congress in 1954. He spoke and campaigned across the country, defending the Eisenhower administration's record and bringing its message to the people.

As a result of his many duties, Dick Nixon was never able to spend as much time at home as he would have liked. The task of looking after the house they now owned near Washington was left to Pat, as were the many details of the education and raising of their two daughters. Still, whenever he could, Dick Nixon made certain he took his meals with his family, set aside some time for short outings, and also checked the girls' homework once in a while.

In 1956, during the Republican National Convention in San Francisco, the sudden illness of his father called him to La Habra, California, where his parents were then living. Frank Nixon, then seventy-seven years old, fought a gallant battle, but he died in September, 1956, just two months before his son and Dwight D. Eisenhower won their campaign for reelection as Vice President and President of the United States. Governor Adlai Stevenson, this time running with Senator Estes Kefauver, was defeated, the vote being thirty-five million to twenty-six million.

During his terms as Vice President, Richard Nixon traveled to fifty-four countries, covering over 160,000 miles, and, as he once boasted, meeting and talking "with some 35 presidents, 9 prime ministers, 5 kings, 2 emperors, and the Shah of Iran." His tasks as a roving diplomat were to represent President Eisenhower, to explain American policies, to clear up misunderstandings between the United States and certain foreign lands, to patch up differences between rulers of other countries, and to show good will.

Late in 1953, he undertook a seventy-two day tour of Asia, visiting Korea, Japan, Indo-China, Burma, and more than a dozen other nations. This trip was hailed as a huge success for several reasons. Instead of meeting only with the ruling figures of the countries he visited, Richard Nixon made it a point to go out and meet the people in the street—laborers, students, even hostile demonstrators. Another reason for the success lay in his careful planning, and his study of a country's problems before his visit. This helped him to explain American views and it also gave him an insight into the ideas of his hosts. Finally, he usually persuaded Pat to accompany him. With her simplicity and grace, Mrs. Nixon won friends for the United States wherever she went.

Not all the Vice President's trips abroad were enjoyable and successful, however. There were times of discomfort and sometimes even danger. On one occasion, in Latin America, he and Pat nearly lost their lives. In the spring of 1958, the Nixons went on a good will trip to South America. After visiting Argentina and several other countries, they arrived in Lima, Peru. There, a group of communists and communist sympathizers made things very uncomfortable for them. When Vice President Nixon went to a large university in the city, stones were thrown at him as he talked to the students and leftist members of the crowd spat on him.

This was only the beginning. When the Nixons arrived at the airport which serves Caracas, the capital of Venezuela, a well-planned attempt was made to insult the Vice Presi-

White House Photos

Richard Nixon married Patricia Ryan on June 21, 1940. Mrs. Nixon is shown here in an official White House portrait as First Lady.

White House Photos

Richard Nixon in the South Pacific during World War II

OPPOSITE: Naval Lieutenant Richard M. Nixon, J.G., 1942
United Press International

MR. AND MRS. RICHARD M. NIXON AND PATRICIA

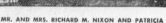

"I pledge myself to serve you faithfully;

To act in the best interests of all of you;

To work for the re-dedication of the United States
of America as a land of opportunity for your children and mine;

To resist with all my power the encroachments of foreign isms
upon the American way of life;

To preserve our sacred heritages, in the name of my buddies and
your loved ones, who died that these might endure;

To devote my full energies to service for you while opposing
regimentation of you;

To remain always humble in the knowledge of your trust in me."

Richard M. Nixon

ELECT

RICHARD M.

NIXON

WORLD WAR II VETERAN

YOUR
CONGRESSMAN

White House Photos

Material from Richard Nixon's first campaign. He won seat in the House of
Representatives in November, 1946.

Some of the freshman Congressmen in Washington in 1947. Richard Nixon is standing next to John F. Kennedy.

Congressman Richard Nixon, his wife Pat, and their daughter Tricia at the
Tidal Basin in Cherry Blossom Time

Senator Richard Nixon, and
his wife and daughters in
1950. Julie joined the family
in 1948.

Republican Party Presidential candidate Dwight D. Eisen-hower and his running mate Senator Richard Nixon at Fraser, Colorado, in 1952

Vice President Richard Nixon with his family on Election Day, 1952

The Nixon brothers, Edward, Donald, and Richard, in Washington, 1952

Hannah and Frank Nixon with their granddaughters in 1952

Mrs. Richard Nixon and daughters

President Dwight D. Eisenhower, his grandson David, and Vice President Richard Nixon and Julie view the Inaugural Parade from the Presidential reviewing stand, 1957.

Vice President Richard Nixon, his wife and daughters at the Inaugural Ball, 1957

Richard Nixon relaxes at Griffith Stadium, 1958.

Photo Trends

Vice President Richard Nixon and a Moroccan schoolboy experience a joyful moment during a good will tour of the African nations, 1957.

The four Nixons on Tricia's sixteenth birthday

White House Photos

The Nixon family in their New York apartment during the late sixties

TOP: Chief Justice Earl Warren administers the oath of office to Richard Nixon, January 20, 1969, while Patricia Nixon holds the family Bibles for her husband. BOTTOM: President and Mrs. Richard Nixon photographed in the White House with their daughters and sons-in-law, Julie and David Eisenhower (left) and Tricia and Edward Cox (right).

dent and the United States, which he represented officially. When he and his wife came off the plane, they saw a hostile crowd on the balcony of the airport terminal. The mob began shouting and screaming so violently that Vice President Nixon decided not to wait around for any airport ceremonies but to go directly to the limousines. As Pat and he passed under the balcony on which the crowd stood, a band began to play the Venezuelan national anthem. Out of respect for their hosts, the Nixons stood while the crowd on the balcony showered them with spit until their clothes were covered with filth. "The police did absolutely nothing," the Vice President later wrote.

The Nixon party finally reached the official cars for the ride into town where they were to take part in a ceremony honoring Simón Bolívar, the great Latin-American hero. On the twelve-mile trip into the city, the Vice President's car was cut off frequently by reckless drivers who sped in and out of the motorcade. Several times, the official automobiles were stopped dead by roadblocks consisting of cars and trucks placed across the highway. When this happened, hundreds of men armed with rocks and steel pipes attacked the limousines. In the entire Nixon party there were only twelve Secret Service men to protect the Vice President, his wife, and those traveling with them. As was the case at the airport, the Venezuelan police did little to help. Car windows were shattered and the Venezuelan Foreign Minister, who was traveling in the same vehicle with Richard Nixon, sustained an injury to his eye. There was so much spit on the windshield that it was necessary to use the wipers.

The motorcade was again under way and headed for the ceremony when Richard Nixon made an important decision. He ordered the cars to go to the American Embassy instead of to the original destination. It was lucky for the whole party that he did this. Near the site of the planned observance, police found hundreds of bombs which, they later proved, the communists were going to use in an assassination attempt against the Vice President of the United States.

Meanwhile, when President Eisenhower heard of the dangerous incidents, he ordered United States Army and Marine units alerted to be flown into Venezuela to bring the Nixon party out safely. This was not necessary, however. Responsible political leaders in Venezuela condemned the mistreatment of their distinguished guests, as did fair-minded citizens and newspaper personnel. Before he left Venezuela, Richard Nixon announced: "I came to Venezuela as a friend and I leave as a friend."

When the Nixons returned safely to Washington, they were greeted by a crowd of fifteen thousand persons, including President Eisenhower, who took the unusual step of meeting the Vice-President's plane at the airport.

This was not the last time that the Vice President had foreign adventures which became front page news all over the world. In 1959, he went to Russia as President Eisenhower's personal representative in connection with the first American exhibit held in that country. The exhibition was designed to show the Russian people how Americans lived, what they worked at, how they relaxed, and what they ate. The displays were set up in a park in Moscow and included a model American home similar to thousands built in the United States every year.

For weeks before the trip, Dick Nixon prepared himself thoroughly. He studied current conditions in Russia, talked to experts on the subject, and memorized a few key phrases of the Russian language. He was particularly careful to learn as much as he could about the head of the country, Nikita Khrushchev.

This was a wise thing to do, since Premier Khrushchev was a tough and opinionated dictator who loved to hear himself talk and did not care who was interrupted as long as he had his say. As a young communist, working for Joseph Stalin, he had earned the nickname "Butcher of the Ukraine" because of his cruelty to the people of that region.

By the time he was ready to take off for Moscow, the Vice President was well prepared. He and his party arrived in Moscow on a July afternoon in 1959, after a flight of some ten hours from Washington in an Air Force jet. Once he was settled in his quarters at the American Embassy in Moscow, the Vice President asked his wife to accompany him and, together, they went for a walk on the streets of Moscow.

The following morning, he and an interpreter and a member of his party went on a private tour of the city. He met the laborers, clerks, and customers at a big fruit-and-vegetable market he visited. This brought back memories of his days in his father's market in Whittier. For an hour, Dick Nixon chatted with the friendly Muscovites through his interpreter, exchanging stories about life in the United States with them and inviting them to view the American exhibition, as thousands of Russians already had. As he was leaving, a storekeeper gave him a large bunch of flowers which he had bought by asking members of the crowd to chip in. The man explained that this was their way of showing friendship for the United States.

Although he was a success with the people, Richard Nixon did not hit it off too well with Premier Khrushchev. One of the activities planned for the Vice-President's trip consisted of his greeting the Russian leader and guiding him on a tour of the exhibit, which covered several hundred thousand square feet. At one point, while standing in front of television cameras, Khrushchev began to attack American governmental policies, the American standard of living, and some of his other favorite targets, including Richard Nixon himself. This was a surprise, since men in high government positions usually behave like gentlemen, especially to their foreign guests.

Walking into the kitchen of the model American home, Khrushchev continued to speak in an insulting manner. The Russian shook his fist, poked his finger into the Vice-President's chest and proclaimed that Americans were warmongers. Dick Nixon recognized that Khrushchev's temper tantrum was really a well-planned act of propaganda in front of television cameras, newspaper photographers, reporters, and both Russian and American visitors and workers at the exhibition. He kept cool but knew he had to reply to the wild charges. In his old debating style, Richard Nixon gave it right back to his antagonist, point for point, while assuring him that he had come to Russia in peace to promote understanding.

When the "Kitchen Debate," as this meeting was later called, got down to personalities, Khrushchev referred to Nixon as a big lawyer, far removed from the ordinary people, while he himself was a former coal miner who knew what it was like to work hard for a living. Nixon told Khrushchev of his early life in California as the son of a grocery-store operator. "Oh, all shopkeepers are thieves," Khrushchev declared flatly. Nixon thought quickly and remembered something he had seen earlier that day while he was touring the government-owned shopping area of Moscow. "Thieving happens everywhere," he said. "Even in the store I visited this morning, I saw people weighing food after they had bought it from the State." Khrushchev had no answer for this.

At the end of the tour, Khrushchev and Nixon toasted each other with wine made from the grapes of California. The Vice President wished that his host might live to be a hundred years old. The foxy Premier remarked that when he was ninety-nine, they could continue their discussion, and Nixon replied, "You mean that at ninety-nine, you will still be in power with no free elections?"

In the days which followed, Nixon and Khrushchev got down to hours of serious talking, exchanging ideas and positions in order that they might understand each other better. The Vice President was also allowed to travel across Russia, stopping in Leningrad and several other important cities. At the end of his stay, according to an agreement which had been made between the two countries, he was permitted to address the Russian people over TV, something no other American official had ever done. The Vice President told his audience that the United States wanted peace but that it did not want to be conquered by communism and so was forced to remain militarily strong.] He also urged that both countries be as friendly to each other as the Russian citizens had been to him.

When he left Russia, the Vice President traveled to Warsaw with his party. There he was met by a huge crowd of 250,000 Poles who cheered him wildly. When he returned to the United States, he found that his Kitchen Debate had increased his popularity with the American people, who always admire a good and fair fighter.

By the end of his second term as Vice President, Richard Nixon could look back with modest pride upon the position he had gained for himself in forty-seven years. All his life, he had been a winner. As he had won honors in school, so he had won elections in 1946, 1948, and 1950 on his own, and in 1952 and 1956 with Dwight Eisenhower. Any player who bats five for five is usually a winner in any ball game. Richard Milhous Nixon seemed unbeatable.

But in 1960, he was faced with the toughest challenger for public office he had encountered up to that time—John F. Kennedy of Massachusetts. While Nixon's career had soared during the 1950's, so had Kennedy's. In 1952, when Nixon was winning the Vice Presidency, Kennedy was taking the Massachusetts Senate seat away from veteran Henry Cabot Lodge, Jr., by a wide margin of votes. In 1956, Senator John Kennedy was mentioned as a possible Vice-Presidential candidate on the Democratic ticket with Governor Adlai Stevenson. He would have been very pleased with this honor but it went instead to Senator Kefauver. Kennedy was reelected to the Senate in 1958 by the largest margin any candidate had ever received in Massachusetts.

The eight years during which Richard Nixon served as Vice President had made him one of the best-known persons in the country and, according to his supporters, one of the best-prepared potential successors to Dwight D. Eisenhower as President of the United States. He had gained experience in government work of all kinds. He knew the rules of the game of government and was familiar with most of the players. For two terms, he had shared in daily confidential briefings on the state of the nation and the world. With his record of background and performance, Vice President Nixon was the logical choice for his party.

Returning to Chicago for the Republican National Convention in July of 1960, eight years after his surprising nomination as Eisenhower's running mate, Richard Nixon became his party's candidate for the Presidency. After listening to all available advice, he selected Henry Cabot Lodge, Jr., as his Vice-Presidential choice.

Meanwhile, in Los Angeles, the Democrats had picked Senator John F. Kennedy as their candidate. This was a very important decision because JFK, as he was affectionately called, was a Roman Catholic and only the second member of this religious group to win the Democratic nomination. The first Roman Catholic, Governor Alfred E. Smith of New York, had been defeated in the election of 1928, and many people believed that this defeat was at least partly due to his religion. There was fear that some people might vote against JFK for reasons of bigotry.

As Senator Kennedy's running mate, the Democratic National Convention named Senator Lyndon B. Johnson of Texas. Senator Johnson was a nationally known figure whose genius as a legislative leader had been relied on by President Eisenhower (even though the two were of different parties) for the passage of much important legislation.

From July to November, 1960, the candidates went through the grueling ordeal of campaigning. By plane, helicopter, train, bus, and automobile, they stumped the country, shaking hands, making speeches, sampling the local food, taking part in the local customs, and, above all, getting their ideas across to the people. Everywhere they went, several dozen reporters traveled along with each, taking note of what they said, how they looked, how the crowds responded. This was quickly relayed back to their newspapers, magazines, radio, or TV stations, to be edited and presented to the people of the nation and the world. No other person is so interviewed, analyzed, talked about, photographed, and just plain prodded, shaken, and poked at as an American Presidential candidate. Fortunately, this lasts only for a few months, but during that time, a man is tested in many ways and much is discovered about him.

In the 1960 campaign, Richard Nixon encountered many difficulties. For one thing, he caught the flu and this weakened him greatly, reducing his usual zest and energy. Yet he continued to work as hard as before, even with a great loss of weight and stamina. He also hurt his knee on a trip to North Carolina when he banged it against a car door. He ignored the injury for a week until the pain became so great that he had to enter a hospital for treatment. This, naturally, cut down on the time he had expected to spend campaigning.

The high point of the 1960 Presidential campaign was a series of four debates between Kennedy and Nixon beginning in late September. Many people advised the Vice President not to engage in this unprecedented contest. He was better known than Senator Kennedy throughout the land; why give his opponent greater exposure before the public? But Dick Nixon had made an excellent reputation in high school and college on the debate team. He had taken on Congressman Jerry Voorhis and become a California Congressman; and he had taken on Premier Khrushchev and become a famous world figure. Debating had been good to Dick Nixon. And, besides, he was as "Irish" as JFK and loved a good verbal battle as much as anyone.

In September of 1960, for the first time in history, two Presidential candidates met before a television audience to argue their differences for the voters of the United States. No one knows how many people watched the first encounter, but some say that over seventy million were tuned in that night.

The Vice President was not at his best during the first debate. In fact, when the broadcast ended, his mother telephoned to ask him if he was well. He was then quite a few pounds underweight. Writing about the event some months later, Richard Nixon said that although he may not have looked as fit as he usually did, "I had never felt better mentally before any important appearance than I did before the first debate."

In the three remaining debates, Dick Nixon looked better

than he had in the first one and was conceded to have held his own for the most part. But he had an extremely attractive, brilliant, and witty opponent in JFK. A strong campaigner, the Senator from Massachusetts traveled throughout the land, carrying his message of better government and a better life for all. The two men presented a very difficult choice for the American voter.

On election night, the results were still in doubt. It was not until the following day that Richard Nixon knew that he had lost the closest Presidential election in the twentieth century. Out of every thousand voters in the country, 497 chose John Kennedy while 495 voted for Richard Nixon. (The other eight votes went to minor party candidates.) More people turned out for this election than for any other in American history. The actual vote was 34,227,096 for Kennedy and 34,107,646 for Nixon.

Many reasons have been offered for the defeat of Richard Nixon. One of the most important is that the television debates hurt him and helped Kennedy. Polls taken after the election showed that millions of voters made up their minds to vote for one candidate or the other on the basis of the debates. And most of these decided for Kennedy, not for the man who had gained so much fame as a noted debater.

Another reason offered for Nixon's defeat was the fact that Dwight Eisenhower did not campaign very actively for him until toward the end of the contest. This gave many persons the false impression that Ike was not enthusiastic about Nixon's becoming his successor. It was true that Ike did not go on extended speaking tours on Nixon's behalf, but it was not revealed until years later that the President's doctor had informed Nixon that Dwight Eisenhower could well have a fatal heart attack if he took on too much campaigning at this point in his life. Richard Nixon therefore did not ask Ike to throw himself totally into the campaign, and this, no doubt, cost him a good many votes.

By January of 1961, Richard Nixon's career in public life was seemingly ended. One of his last official duties as Vice President was to certify John F. Kennedy as President on the basis of the electoral votes from the states.

After the inauguration of JFK, Richard Nixon and his family left the capital to which they had come fourteen years earlier. The former Vice President returned to California with a great many memories which nearly—but not quite—wiped out the overwhelming thought of what he had missed by so little. One of the memories he brought with him was a statement made by President Charles deGaulle of France, whom he admired greatly. A few months earlier, President de Gaulle had described Richard Nixon as "a man upon whom great hopes rest . . . a man who understands the past, but has all the future before him."

CHAPTER VII

RICHARD NIXON had lived for and lived with public office for fourteen years. Now, having lost the race for the Presidency to John F. Kennedy, he was out of political life and felt somewhat lost. Since few persons have ever been in the position of losing the world's most important job, few could understand the former Vice President's predicament. One man, who had lost in not one but two Presidential elections, could understand Richard Nixon's feelings. This was Thomas E. Dewey, twice the Republican Presidential candidate, a former Governor of New York, and a trusted friend of the Nixons. Mr. Dewey advised Richard Nixon not to make any decision about his future for at least a few months.

The Nixon family slowly began to adjust to "civilian" life. One of the biggest dividends of Dick Nixon's release from public service was that he could enjoy more time with Pat and his daughters. Tricia was now fourteen, and Julie was twelve. The children of Californians, and frequent visitors to that state, the Nixon girls were really able to call Washington their second home, since they had grown up in the capital's suburbs. All that was ended, now, as their parents sold their house and moved back to the West Coast. While their new home near Beverly Hills was being built, the family rented a place nearby from a motion-picture executive. When the building was finished, Pat and Dick Nixon could take pleasure in their realization of a dream of over twenty years' duration. They now had a home of their own, with a swimming pool and all the other "extras" which so many Americans hope to acquire "some day," when they achieve success.

Domestic life was very rewarding for the 48-year-old "retired" Vice President. He could talk things over with the girls more regularly, help Pat supervise their education, and go swimming with them in the new family pool. He relaxed a bit more outside his home, too, especially on the golf course. He had picked up the game as Vice President, partly because President Eisenhower was then one of the world's most devoted golfers. On Labor Day, 1961, Dick achieved the golfer's goal—a hole in one!

While he was becoming accustomed to having more control over his domestic and personal life, Richard Nixon was also reviewing his future from an economic point of view. He needed a good deal of money to give his family all that he wanted them to have, so he considered the many job offers he received very carefully. He was asked to take the presidency of business firms and universities, but he decided instead to join the Los Angeles firm of Adams, Duque, and Hazeltine. The Nixon name was soon attracting a great deal of legal business, and Dick Nixon himself was practicing law with all the zest and care for detail that he had expended in Whittier before the war. His financial success surprised him a bit as the money came fairly rolling in. In the first year after he left public service, his income tax alone was double what his salary had been as Vice President.

Richard Nixon also became a newspaperman, writing a column which appeared in dozens of papers all across the country for a year or so. This gave him the opportunity to express his views on public issues and also to keep his own name before the American people. He also agreed to write a book about his experiences as Vice President. For seven months, he labored over the task. The result was/Six Crises, a work which described six of the great events in which he had participated during the years from 1948 to 1960. It includes accounts of the Hiss-Chambers affair; the "Checkers Speech"; President Eisenhower's illnesses; the episode in Caracas, Venezuela; the "Kitchen Debate" with Premier Khrushchev; and the election campaign of 1960. This volume of memories, which is nearly five hundred pages long, became a national best-seller and it remains an important historical source. The book is dedicated to Pat because, as the author wrote, "she also ran."

In the first year or so following his withdrawal from the active political scene, Richard Nixon was called upon from time to time to advise public leaders. One of these occasions occurred when President John F. Kennedy invited him to the White House for consultation after the unsuccessful invasion of Cuba by American-aided Cuban exiles. The two men talked for over an hour about this episode, now known as the "Bay of Pigs" invasion, and Richard Nixon gave his political foe of less than a year before the best advice he could. Later, he performed another service for the President and his country, telephoning Republican leaders all over the United States and urging them to rally behind their President in this crisis. He did not think it was right to use this occasion to criticize the wisdom of the Democratic party and its leaders.

Of course, when he did not think it would hurt his country or weaken its position in the world, Richard Nixon was quick to condemn JFK or any office-holding Democrat for policies he considered unsuitable for America's needs.

The year 1961 was a significant one for the United States. In addition to the Cuban invasion which failed, Premier Khrushchev, Nixon's debating opponent, took a bold gamble and broke a previous agreement between Russia and the Western allies by sealing off East from West Berlin. Barbed wire and, later, concrete walls were erected to prevent East Germans from fleeing to freedom in West Berlin. At the same time, on the other side of the world, communists increased pressure against the free government of South Vietnam in Southeast Asia. President Kennedy reacted to the Asian crisis by sending military experts to study the situation. The following year, about five thousand American soldiers were sent to protect South Vietnam. By 1963, the number had increased to more than sixteen thousand. President Kennedy was determined to do everything possible to prevent a communist takeover of this vital area of the world.

Private life had its attractive side for Richard Nixon, but, after so many years of public service, it was only natural for him to look forward to a return to the power and influence which goes with holding high government office. Shortly after he left the Vice Presidency, some of his friends began to urge him to run for governor of California in 1962. The more he thought about it, the more the idea of becoming chief executive of the second most populous state in the Union grew on him. After talking it over with his family, friends, and political allies, he decided to take the plunge, living up to a statement he had once made to a reporter: "I'm always willing to take a chance. I think that has been the mark of my political career."

The campaign for California governor was a bruising one. It began with a bitter primary fight within the Republican party itself. Richard Nixon won the nomination, but the struggle left many wounds and probably contributed to his defeat during the general election in November, 1962. Governor Edmund "Pat" Brown had polled 3,000,000 votes to 2,700,000 for Nixon. It was a terrific blow, perhaps even worse than the defeat in the Presidential race of 1960. It seemed as if Richard Nixon's whole world had caved in.

The morning after election day, he appeared before a press conference to give his reactions to the affair. Throwing his usual caution away, Dick Nixon blew his top and "told the press off," accusing many journalists of unfair reporting. Toward the end of his remarks, he added: "I want you to know—just how much you're going to be missing. You won't have Nixon to kick around anymore, because, gentlemen, this is my last press conference."

As usual, no one was neutral when it came to Richard Nixon. His supporters defended his angry farewell by saying that the press deserved it because of its failure to report the facts of the campaign fairly. On the other hand, his opponents claimed that Nixon was just being a "sore loser" who blamed the newspapers for his own mistakes. But that was it. Richard Nixon was finished with political life—in his own mind. And many in the news field agreed with him that he was finished as a leading American politician. In fact, a major television network broadcast a "special" called the "Political Obituary of Richard Nixon." Among the guests on the program was Alger Hiss, released from prison after serving his term for perjury. The broadcast backfired. Instead of marking the end of Nixon's political career, the program created a great deal of sympathy for him. The public sent thousands of letters to the American Broadcasting Company (ABC) to protest the appearance of Mr. Hiss and to complain of what was considered bad taste in presenting the show. The Senate of the State of Illinois demanded that the network apologize for it. One Democratic state Senator said: "I was never an admirer of Nixon and voted against him," but he regarded the television presentation as a "vicious thing." Other Americans, including more government officials, declared that the TV stations had the right to present their programs as they saw fit, without outside interference.

Even though Richard M. Nixon was no longer in office, he was still a figure of great importance. When he spoke, his words were widely reported and read. This, of course, often brought him threatening letters and other forms of abuse, particularly from unbalanced persons. He had come to expect this, along with the handshakes and requests for autographs from well-wishers. In April, 1963, however, he escaped a situation which could have been as serious as any he had ever encountered. While he was in Dallas, Texas, on business, a deranged former Marine named Lee Harvey Oswald decided to go meet him. Oswald had defected to the Soviet Union after his military service, had married a Russian woman, and had returned to the United States as a devoted communist. According to his wife, he resented Richard Nixon's frequent attacks on the policies of Fidel Castro's government in Cuba. On this particular morning in April, 1963, Oswald had loaded a pistol and was dressing for his trip to see Nixon when his wife stopped him from going out. Richard Nixon knew nothing of this until many months later. At the time, he and his family were occupied with a very important decision.

After a great deal of discussion, the Nixons decided to leave California, and the home they had built there, and settle in New York. In June of 1963, after a memorable farewell party in Los Angeles given by some thirteen hundred friends, the Nixon family left their home state. They took up residence in Manhattan in a twelve-room apartment overlooking Central Park, and quickly adjusted to living in the area.

Richard Nixon joined a famous New York law firm, which came to be called Nixon, Mudge, Rose, Guthrie, and Alexander. He was admitted to the New York State Bar and could then practice in the courts of the state. The man who had been brought up in the West, partially educated in the South, and spent time during his Navy service in the Midwest, was now settled in the Northeast. He also traveled throughout the United States and to many parts of the world on his firm's business, meeting again many of the people he had known when he was Vice President. He further did what other serious Americans tried to do, he associated himself with worthy causes in order to help improve society. He became chairman of the Boys' Clubs of America, and he offered his time and financial support to other civic and charitable groups.

November of 1963 brought Richard Nixon to Dallas, Texas, again. He flew back to New York on the twenty-second of the month, as President Kennedy, his wife, and their official party arrived in the city. When Nixon landed in New York, he heard that President Kennedy had been assassinated in the city he had just left. The assassin was Lee Harvey Oswald. The event shook Nixon badly, because of the friendship he felt for the former President as well as his grief for John Kennedy's family and the country. As a result of this tragedy, Vice President Lyndon B. Johnson became the thirty-sixth President of the United States.

Although he had announced that he would never again seek political office, Richard Nixon was certainly not finished with politics. When President Lyndon Johnson and his running mate, Senator Hubert H. Humphrey of Minnesota, were nominated by the Democrats in 1964, Nixon became a campaigner in behalf of Republican Presidential candidate Senator Barry M. Goldwater of Arizona and his running mate, Congressman William Miller of New York. With his customary energy, Nixon put his prestige and his time on the line for these and other Republican candidates across the country. He logged fifty thousand miles in a month and a half during the fall of 1964.

Senator Goldwater was disastrously defeated. Lyndon Johnson received 61 per cent of the popular vote, which was a record-breaking figure. Not only that, Republican candidates everywhere were badly beaten. The House and Senate now both had twice as many members who were Democrats as Republicans.

Politically, it looked as if Richard Nixon could do nothing right. He had played a major part in three election disasters—1960, 1962, and 1964. It is true that he had not been a candidate for office in 1964, but he had been a leading campaigner and had to share heavily in the blame. Along with the impression of being a loser, though, Richard Nixon also carried with him the loyalty of thousands of Republicans who knew he had done his best to help them.

During the years which followed the 1964 election, things did not go well with the United States. The country became more and more involved in Vietnam as the 16,000 servicemen President Kennedy had sent to the country by 1963 grew under President Johnson to 549,000. The United States was engaged in a large-scale war, suffering hundreds of casualties every week. This contributed to discontent at home. Racial problems, the rising crime rate, and the existence of wide-spread poverty were some of the main domestic concerns of the second half of the 1960's. The government under the guidance of President Johnson tried to solve these problems. The Vietnam war was carried on vigorously on land and in the air; laws protecting the rights of minorities in the country were passed and energetically enforced; money was voted to solve the crime problems;

and anti-poverty programs were begun to better feed, house, and educate the disadvantaged.

Unfortunately, many Americans did not think that the government was doing enough in any area. New forms of protest began to arise as demonstrators filled the streets and picketed colleges, businesses, and government offices in support of their causes. Rioting also broke out, leading to deaths, injuries, and continued discontent. America in the late 1960's was not a happy country. Everything seemed to be going wrong. Richard Nixon was aware of all this more than most people and worried over it a great deal.

Life went well for him personally. His yearly income averaged about $200,000 as a lawyer, and he made over $200,000 on the sale of his book, *Six Crises,* alone. When he had time, he enjoyed going to the country clubs to which he belonged, as well as entertaining friends in town and being entertained in return. He watched proudly as his daughters grew into young women, attending college, "coming out" as debutantes in society, and dating young men. In October, 1966, the Nixons' young daughter, Julie, told them that she had been on a date with David Eisenhower, grandson of the former President. These family joys meant much to Richard Nixon, but he still had a great deal of energy left over for public concerns. Even while he enjoyed his law career and the rewards it brought, he missed the drama of political life and the chance to do something about America's problems.

When the 1966 campaign for Congress started, he was again ready to offer his services to his party. As he had done for years, the former Vice President traveled across dozens of states, making speeches in support of candidates he favored, and appearing at fund-raising dinners. It is estimated that he raised millions of dollars for the Republican cause by his willingness to fly almost anywhere in the country for the sake of his party.

The year 1966 was a triumphant one for the Republicans, who won fifty seats in Congress and scored sizable victories in state elections, too. Richard Nixon had the right to be proud of the part he had played in the election. Surveys later showed that those candidates who had Nixon's backing had a better chance of winning than those who did not.

During the following years, articles began to appear in newspapers and magazines, speculating over Nixon's political future. Many of the writers recognized that he still had a great deal of influence, but most also remarked that, personally, Dick Nixon was a loser. He had lost races for the Presidency and the governorship of California and, in such high politics, few men get a second chance. The American people thought highly of him, it was said, but they obviously did not want him as a leader. Nixon can't win, was the way this was written.

The year 1967 contained three moving events in the lives of the Nixons. First, Hannah Nixon died, casting the family into grief. His loss of a loving mother, a staunch friend, and a sage political ally was a deep blow to Richard Nixon. Second, Julie Nixon and David Eisenhower announced their engagement, bringing a note of joy to the year. Third, Richard Nixon made his decision to seek the Republican nomination for Presidential candidate in 1968.

During 1967, Nixon began planning his strategy for the

upcoming campaign, following the tactics he and his old friend and manager, Murray Chotiner, had adopted back in 1946, when Nixon first ran for public office. Many of his former allies in political life began to rally around him, and he also attracted a new group of younger men who believed in his ideas. Early in 1968, he made his decision public by announcing that he was a candidate and would run in primary elections throughout the country.

The most important thing was to erase the feeling that he was a loser. This he hoped to do by winning indisputable victories in primaries throughout the nation. The earliest of the fifteen primaries held in 1968 was in New Hampshire. This state is usually a Republican stronghold, but whether or not it was a stronghold of Nixon Republicans was another question.

The answer came in the middle of March, when the people of New Hampshire went to the polls for their primary election. Nixon totaled over eighty thousand votes, which was more than any other person running in such an election in that state had ever received. Governor Rockefeller of New York came in second with eleven thousand votes.

The vote in this small but significant state "proved" to many Republicans that Nixon still could win an election. What was very pleasing to Nixon was the fact that several thousand Democrats wrote in his name on the Democratic ballot. He knew that he needed the votes of millions of Democrats if he were to win the Presidency, so a special part of his campaign was directed toward them.

After New Hampshire, Richard Nixon won in other key

primaries, sometimes without opposition from any other Republican candidate. The way people turned out to show support was surprising and satisfying to him. He received 80 per cent of the ballots in Wisconsin, 70 per cent in Nebraska, and 73 per cent in Oregon. Here, too, Democrats were voting for him.

On the Democratic side, the campaign of 1968 began with most people assuming that President Johnson would be a candidate again. Lyndon Johnson's landslide victory of 1964 convinced many Democrats that he was the best possible choice as nominee. Supporters of Senator Eugene McCarthy thought otherwise, however, and campaigned actively for him in New Hampshire. When the returns were tallied, President Johnson had received the most votes in the Democratic primary, but Senator McCarthy was so close that it looked like a Johnson defeat, particularly since President Johnson had scored such a triumph in the 1964 Presidential election.

Two weeks after the New Hampshire primary, President Johnson removed himself as a candidate with the words: "I shall not seek and I will not accept the nomination of my party for another term. . . ." Mr. Johnson had served in the Presidency for over four years and had decided, with his wife, Lady Bird Johnson, not to run again. Many reasons motivated his decision, including a heart condition which might be worsened by continued stress and a desire to sacrifice himself in an effort to bring about a settlement of the Vietnam war.

The three most important candidates remaining in the race were Vice President Hubert H. Humphrey, Senator

Engene McCarthy, and Senator Robert F. Kennedy of New York. Robert Kennedy was a younger brother of the late President and had served the Kennedy and Johnson administrations as Attorney General until his election as Senator from New York State. Shortly after the New Hampshire primary, Senator Kennedy entered the race for the Democratic nomination for President. During the month of April, Kennedy trailed McCarthy in primaries in Wisconsin, Pennsylvania, and Massachusetts. In May, however, he pulled ahead in Indiana and Nebraska and, in June, Kennedy won a decisive victory over McCarthy in California. While Robert Kennedy and his followers jubilantly celebrated their victory in the California primary, an assassin lay in wait for him. A man called Sirhan Sirhan shot Robert Kennedy to death. The news shocked the nation, which could scarcely believe this murder of a second Kennedy brother.

At their National Convention, held in Chicago in August, 1968, the Democrats chose Hubert H. Humphrey as their candidate. Senator Edmund Muskie of Maine was selected as his running mate. Hubert Humphrey was a likable and energetic liberal, with a reputation as a hard fighter but a fair man. Beating him was going to be no picnic for his Republican opponent.

At the Republican National Convention in Miami, Florida, Richard Nixon was chosen to be his party's candidate. He selected Governor Spiro T. Agnew of Maryland as his running mate. Agnew, son of a Greek immigrant family, was an outspoken lawyer who was fairly new in the political field but who had already earned a reputation as a hard-working governor. Nixon did not know Agnew well. In fact, he had met him for the first time only a few months before. He wanted as his Vice-Presidential nominee a man who was not afraid to take a stand on issues, who had the energy to conduct a strong campaign, and who would not let the opposition disturb him by their attacks. "He's got it," Nixon said of Spiro Agnew, putting all his experience as a judge of men behind his decision.

Every move counted in this election. By picking a man from Maryland as his Vice-Presidential choice, Nixon hoped to weaken the campaign of a strong third-party candidate, Governor George C. Wallace of Alabama. Governor Wallace was extremely popular throughout the South and he was the first candidate of a third party to pose a threat to the two major parties in more than forty years.

In his acceptance speech before the Republican Convention, Richard Nixon spoke of two children. One of these was a child of poverty in 1968: "He is black or he is white, he is Mexican, Italian, Polish. None of that matters. What matters is he is an American child." Nixon continued, "He sleeps the sleep of childhood, he dreams the dreams of a child. And yet when he awakens, he awakens to a living nightmare of poverty, neglect, and despair. He fails in school, he ends up on welfare. For him the American system is one that feeds his stomach and starves his soul."

Then, in one of the few times when he has spoken of himself, Richard Nixon spoke of another child: "He hears a train go by. At night he dreams of faraway places where he'd like to go. It seems like an impossible dream. But he is helped on his journey through life. A father who had to go

to work before he finished the sixth grade sacrificed everything he had so that his sons could go to college. A gentle
Quaker mother, with a passionate concern for peace, quietly
wept when he went to war but she understood why he had
to go. A great teacher, a remarkable football coach, an in-
spirational minister encouraged him on his way. A courageous wife and loyal children stood by him in victory and
also in defeat. And in his chosen profession of politics, there
were scores, then hundreds, then thousands, and then finally
millions who worked for his success."

In this way, Richard Nixon gave credit to all those who
had helped him to achieve his childhood dreams, from his
earliest years until the present moment.

A good many reasons can be given for Dick Nixon's willingness to go through another grueling campaign—his own
ambition, his desire to serve his country, the urging of his
friends, and many others. Perhaps his motives could best be
summed up in a statement he made when he first announced
publicly that he would be a candidate. He said that he knew
America faced many problems, but he also said: "I believe
I have found some answers."

Now that he had the nomination, he began to share his
answers with the voters, to convince them that they were
the right ones. In order to do this, he felt that it was necessary to communicate with the American people as directly
and fully as possible. In his life as a politician, Richard
Nixon had been born at about the same time that the television industry came into being. In 1946, when he first
entered politics, there were only eight thousand families in

the United States with TV sets. By the time of the Checkers Speech of 1952, over fifteen million families owned sets. About forty-five million families had sets for the debates of Nixon with JFK in 1960, and by 1968 over 95 per cent of American homes boasted a set. Nixon had taken advantage of this new tool in promoting his career, as his father had taken advantage of the automobile and its need for fuel when it was first becoming popular.

In a way, Richard Nixon was a product of television. He had saved his political life in 1952 by the Checkers Speech, and he had lost it eight years later through the Kennedy-Nixon debates. Now, he wanted to make sure that TV would be an aid, not a hindrance to him.

While most Americans will walk down to the corner of their street if they know a Presidential candidate is expected to pass by, they will not go much farther. After a hard day's work, they want to relax by reading the newspaper, listening to the radio, or watching television. Many candidates for public office do not realize that by using television or radio they can reach millions of voters at one time, whereas by barnstorming for months over the country they might only manage to talk to one or two million persons altogether.

While he worked hard, Nixon did not exhaust himself physically campaigning in 1968 as he had in 1960. He followed a schedule which would tire most people out in a few days, but which for him was just right. And he remained calm as he talked to the people over the radio in straightforward language about the nation's problems as he saw them. When he appeared on TV, he was well rested and relaxed, speaking informally without notes—which showed people how familiar he was with his subject.

Still, the public opinion polls showed that the election was going to be very close. The effect of the candidacy of George Wallace on the results could not be predicted. When the ballots were finally tallied, they showed that Nixon had defeated Hubert Humphrey by a thin margin of 500,000 votes. Nixon's total was 31,770,237, with 31,270,-533 for Humphrey and 9,906,141 for Wallace. It was a close decision, although not as close as the one in 1960.

Richard Milhous Nixon had won the greatest race of his life but he realized he could not relax and enjoy his victory. After the election, the Nixon family went on vacation, but for the "President-elect," as the winner is called, it was a working holiday. Between November of 1968 and January, 1969, Richard Nixon spent his time selecting his cabinet and other advisers, preparing his program for the next four years, being briefed on the latest developments in world conditions by the outgoing Johnson administration, and writing his inaugural address. Richard and Pat Nixon also had the pleasure of taking part in the wedding of their daughter, Julie, to David Eisenhower, President Eisenhower's grandson, in December, 1968.

Shortly before his inauguration, Richard Nixon was guest of honor at a homecoming celebration given by thousands of his California friends. What made it especially enjoyable was the presence of many of his relatives, friends, and former football teammates. At the ceremony, he was awarded a football letter from Whittier College, and he was also given the bench he had warmed for so long while he was a team member.

The Nixons decided to give up their New York residence, and they purchased a home at Key Biscayne, Florida. This would allow them a secluded retreat from the pressures of Washington during their years in the White House.

In a speech made after his election, Richard Nixon remarked that, while he was campaigning, he had seen a young woman carrying a sign that read: "BRING US TOGETHER AGAIN." The girl was invited to attend the inaugural ceremonies because her sign gave the President-elect the inspiration for the motto which became the main theme of his administration—"Forward Together."

CHAPTER VIII

❧

Mᴏɴᴅᴀʏ, ᴊᴀɴᴜᴀʀʏ 20, 1969, was the day on which Richard Nixon gave up the status of private citizen once more to enter what one former President had called the "splendid misery" of the Presidency. On the morning of inauguration day, Nixon left his Washington hotel early in order to attend a prayer service held in the State Department building. Then, escorted by motorcycle police, he returned to his hotel. At about ten-thirty, he and Pat drove to the White House for the customary visit with President and Mrs. Lyndon B. Johnson. For a short time, the incoming tenants of the 132-room mansion on Pennsylvania Avenue chatted informally over coffee with the outgoing occupants. Then, President Johnson and President-elect Nixon entered the first automobile of a large motorcade and drove to the Capitol building.

On the steps of the Capitol, Chief Justice Earl Warren administered the oath of office to the new President, who rested his hand on two family Bibles held by his wife. The Bibles were both open to the page on which Isaiah's prophecy was written: ". . . they shall beat their swords into plowshares and their spears into pruning hooks; nation shall not lift up sword against nation, neither shall they learn war any more."

After taking the oath, Richard Nixon, now thirty-seventh President of the United States, rose, looked earnestly out over the assembled officials, guests, and fellow-citizens, and began his Inaugural Address. In this speech he was brief, as always, holding the talk to only seventeen minutes. He promised to devote his full energies to peace, stating that the ". . . greatest honor history can bestow is the title of peacemaker." He urged Americans to take as their goal the following ideals: ". . . where peace is unknown, make it welcome; where peace is fragile, make it strong; where peace is temporary, make it permanent." But he also noted that "peace does not come through wishing for it." It was necessary to work with all nations to achieve it.

The President promised to seek justice at home as enthusiastically as he sought peace abroad. This included justice for all, regardless of race or religion. "No man can be truly free," he observed, "while his neighbor is not. To go forward at all is to go forward together."

The Inaugural Address was broadcast over television and radio to several hundred million people around the world. It was analyzed carefully for clues as to what the new administration hoped to accomplish during the next four years.

The swearing-in ceremony and the Inaugural Address are the solemn, formal parts of Presidential inauguration days. After these are completed, the celebrations begin. For President Nixon, the festivities started with a luncheon in the Capitol with his new Cabinet, legislative leaders, and friends. Following this, he and the new First Lady took their places in the lead car of the motorcade which headed the Inaugural parade. When they reached the White House, the Nixons, their family, and friends entered the specially constructed reviewing stand on Pennsylvania Avenue to watch the parade. In spite of the cold weather, 250,000 spectators lined the streets of Washington to view the marchers, while millions watched the event at home on television.

The President stayed through it all, enthusiastically clapping and waving as the floats and bands passed by. Floats representing states, marching bands from the Service Academies, special displays of all kinds captured the attention of on-lookers. Some of the marchers had special significance for the President and the First Lady, who were pleased to see the Whittier High School band lead the California float in honor of the school's best-known graduate and its most-famous teacher.

Not all those present in Washington that Monday in January were Richard Nixon's well-wishers. Thousands of young people, some of them nicknamed "crazies," tried to disrupt the various ceremonies by shouting, throwing things, and shoving through police lines. Demonstrators stormed around the city breaking windows, burning American flags, and painting pro-communist statements on buildings. About eighty young people were arrested on charges of committing various illegal acts. This was the first large-scale opposition demonstration ever to occur during the Inauguration of a President of the United States.

Nevertheless, the mood of the new President remained bright, as the smiles of the paraders, most of whom were young, added to the joys of the day. By early evening, the parade was over and the President and his family entered the White House to dine and prepare for the nighttime functions. That evening, six Inaugural Balls were held in order to accommodate the thousands of persons who wished to attend the festivities. The President and his family visited each ball site, greeting the guests with quips and smiles. Among the thousands who attended these parties were more than sixty of Richard Nixon's relatives, along with hundreds of classmates and friends from all over the country, from California to New York. The balls continued far into the night and it was not until after midnight that the Nixons were able to return to their new home in the White House.

In spite of this, the President was up and at his desk early the following morning. This was the beginning of a rigorous schedule which Richard Nixon set for himself during his years in the Presidential office.

Although there was no such thing as a "typical" day in the life of the President, there were things he came to do regularly. He woke about seven-thirty, had a light breakfast, and left the family quarters of the White House for the Oval Office. His official day began with the reading of a long information summary prepared for him by his staff. This ran to about fifty typewritten pages filled with condensed versions of newspaper stories, editorials, and television and radio programs. The staff had read about sixty newspapers and boiled down the important stories for the President's use. They did the same thing with magazines, condensing articles in more than thirty periodicals at regular intervals. These sources of information supplemented reports given to him orally and in writing by the Federal Bureau of Investigation (FBI), the Central Intelligence Agency (CIA), and other investigative agencies.

By the time he had consumed this massive diet of information, the President was ready for his appointments. Until nearly one in the afternoon, a stream of visitors poured into the Oval Office to talk to him. The Attorney General might come to discuss an anti-crime bill which Congress was considering, or the Secretary of State to present a diplomatic problem, or a foreign visitor to extend the best wishes of his government to the American people.

When the morning appointments ended, the President usually had a quick lunch of fruit, or perhaps cottage cheese covered with catchup. Then, a meeting with his aides might be held to go over the morning's work. If anything needed action, it would be ordered, the President telling one staff member to visit a particular Congressman to ask his support for a bill, for example. Occasionally at this point in his day, the President might take a nap.

At three o'clock, the heavy schedule was renewed, with appointments taking up the afternoon hours. The fifty or sixty persons the President saw on such a day as this came from all walks of life. On a typical schedule, he might meet a beauty queen, a war hero, a handicapped child, a world religious leader, a manufacturer, an entertainer, and a state governor.

The second round of appointments was usually over by six o'clock, after which President Nixon generally wound up his day at the office by giving another set of orders to his staff. At seven-thirty, he would join his wife for dinner, unless they had to attend some function outside the White House or were to be host and hostess for a dinner at home. If he had a free evening, it was apt to be taken up with paper work, done in the family quarters of the White House.

To keep from becoming too isolated within the Executive Mansion, Richard Nixon used the telephone frequently to stay in touch with old friends. He also read some of the latest books, and watched some TV. His greatest TV interest was football. He occasionally went to see his favorite teams at practice and in play, and even discussed plays with the coaches. He liked baseball, too. At night, he and his family sometimes saw a movie, shown right in the White House. Among the films he enjoyed were *Patton* and *Love Story*, and he also liked Westerns. If he had time, he bowled a game or two in the White House alley.

By midnight, Richard Nixon was ready for bed, although he sometimes stayed awake until two, writing and reading. Only a person with great stamina could keep up this kind of schedule for a long time. Sixteen-hour work days, followed on occasion by long evenings at dinners, would exhaust most people very soon.

Among the reasons for President Nixon's ability to withstand his rigorous schedule was his extraordinary self-discipline. He smoked very rarely, drank a martini or a glass of wine only once in a while, and dieted continuously. Richard Nixon loved to eat, but he kept his food intake down in order to stay at his ideal weight of 170 pounds. He enjoyed

Mexican food, as well as steaks, meat loaf, and macadamia nut ice cream. He exercised very little, except for running in place when he got up each morning and some bowling and golf.

A great demand on Richard Nixon's time was entertaining, which he and Pat undertook with greater enthusiasm than any previous first family. The guests included singer Johnny Cash, the Irish Ambassador to the United States, British showman David Frost, preacher Billy Graham, the great musician Duke Ellington, and thousands of others. Richard Nixon showed his appreciation for Duke Ellington by playing "Happy Birthday" on the piano at a seventieth birthday dinner in honor of the "Duke." Ellington's father once served as a butler at the White House and it was especially appropriate that the son should be honored with the Medal of Freedom. Richard Nixon said: "In the royalty of American music, no man swings more or stands higher than the Duke."

Richard Nixon enjoyed being President. And he developed his own style in that office, as all Presidents do. He liked doing the unexpected, popping into a staff member's office for a chat, calling a friend on the telephone. He used his position to do what he—as President—thought he could and should do. On one Thanksgiving, he had 230 elderly people from the Washington area for dinner in the Executive Mansion.

During his White House years, Richard Nixon began the practice of holding religious services in the East Room and inviting hundreds of persons to attend them. These were non-denominational exercises and were held fairly regularly, about every two weeks or so. Ministers, priests, and rabbis from all the major religions were invited to conduct the services, and various choirs were selected to lead the worshippers in singing. After the conclusion of the Sunday morning ritual, President and Mrs. Nixon would greet their guests and enjoy a light breakfast with them.

The Presidency, then, is not all work. Richard Nixon had time to relax from his duties for short periods of time. He and Pat got away from Washington to their home in Key Biscayne when they could, flying to Florida in the *Spirit of '76*, the big Air Force jet placed at the President's disposal. Or they might helicopter to a government-owned Presidential retreat called Camp David in Maryland. The camp had been named years before by President Eisenhower for his grandson, David.

A few months after taking office, Richard Nixon and his wife went house-hunting in their native California. They found a beautiful ranch house built in the Spanish style of architecture near San Clemente. It was located on the beach overlooking the Pacific Ocean and appeared secluded enough to give the Nixons the hideaway they needed while still in the public eye, and would be a perfect place to settle down in eventually. The ranch became known as the "Western White House," and in the area around it devices were set up to allow the President to be in touch with all branches of the government at all times.

A President's holiday is not like that of anyone else. There is no getting away completely from his job at any time. Secret Servicemen are always within close range of the Chief Executive to provide him with as much security as possible. And also nearby is the officer who carries with him a valise containing the secret information necessary for the President to order a counter attack in the event that the United States becomes the nuclear target of an aggressor. This official, who is in the background but who is always present, is a continual reminder of the heavy burdens a President bears.

While on "vacation," President Nixon worked only about half his regular sixteen hours, winding up in the afternoon to allow time for relaxing in the sun, dining in a leisurely fashion, golfing, watching football, reading, or just loafing.

In addition to the fame, prestige, and power which the Presidency of the United States brings, there are more tangible rewards. There is a four year "lease" on the White House with its eighteen acres of grounds and its 132 rooms. There is a salary of $200,000, plus travel and expense allowances of $90,000, funds of nearly $6,000,000 for Secret Service, police, and White House operations, and another $1,500,000 which the President may use as he sees fit for official government purposes. Several Air Force jets (including the *Spirit of '76*), a few helicopters, and a fleet of two dozen cars are also available for White House use.

But with the many rewards of the office, the Presidency is accompanied by three ever-present companions—danger, criticism, and responsibility. Even before his inauguration, Richard Nixon received the usual threats that unbalanced men feel they must make against the lives of famous persons. After he assumed office, it became a common task of the Secret Service to investigate all those who threatened his life. When an explosion in the Senate wing of the Capitol caused great damage to that building, the suggestion was made that the Capitol and the White House might have to be closed to visitors. President Nixon refused to hear of this, at least as far as the White House was concerned, stating that the more than one and a half million persons who toured the Executive Mansion every year could not be denied the right to see "their" building.

Aside from danger, the President lived with the next most unpleasant companion—criticism. As Chief Executive and the head of a civilian and military force of millions, he was required to take the blame for any and all mistakes which occurred in his administration, not just his own. When officials decided to save money by abolishing the Federal government's tea tasters, the tea industry condemned the move and the tea tasters were retained. When Richard Nixon made blunders on his own, he was quickly called to account. Commenting on a man accused of mass murder, the President declared that he was guilty before the trial was over. He was criticized for speaking without thinking, and later admitted that he deserved the criticism. When a judge he selected for appointment to the Supreme Court was accused of having a background that included racial bias, the Senate objected and refused to confirm his choice.

Much of the criticism hurt; in some cases it helped, since it is the job of newspapers, magazines, radio, TV, and citizens to make as much noise as possible if they feel that some policy or action of their government deserves censure. President Nixon liked to quote one of President Harry Truman's favorite sayings about the man in the Oval Office: "If you can't take the heat, get out of the kitchen."

Danger and criticism go inevitably with the job of President, as does the third companion—responsibility. In explaining this, a scholar named Clinton Rossiter once wrote that the President is "a kind of magnificent lion who can roam widely and do great deeds so long as he does not try to break loose from his broad reservation." When an event which touches on his area of responsibility takes place, the President must react. He has no other choice. "The buck stops here," President Harry Truman once said, pointing to his desk.

In the case of Richard Nixon's Presidency, this has involved doing many things which were not popular or always pleasant, but which had to be done. When Post Office workers went on strike for the first time in American history, for example, President Nixon declared a national emergency and replaced the strikers with active and reserve members of the Armed Forces until the postal employees agreed to return to work. Again, when prices and wages got to the point where they were causing serious inflation which was damaging the American economy, he used his Presidential authority to place a freeze on wages and set up a board to keep the nation's economic life from being hurt by rapid increases in prices.

As a citizen and a public official, Richard Nixon had always complained of inefficiency in government. As President, he was given the chance to do something about this. After much study, he recommended to Congress that various Federal agencies be merged in order to streamline the government. Wherever he himself could order changes to improve the workings of the Executive branch, he did so right away. The Federal government had previously approved loans to cities and states for purposes such as building more housing, but local and state officials soon discovered that they had to hire experts to fill out all the forms needed just to apply for the money. To secure aid for housing under one program, for example, it was necessary to fill out forms containing 286 items. The Nixon administration cut down paperwork such as this drastically, making it much easier to apply for aid. In another instance, it once took ninety-six days to get approval or disapproval of a project; this was cut to five.

In other ways, too, a quiet revolution went on. When Richard Nixon took office, in January of 1969, less than three million persons were receiving food stamps to help satisfy their needs. The President ordered that the hunger problem be attacked head-on. Two years later, the number of people being helped with food stamps had grown to some nine million. Feeding the poor of America became a high goal on the President's list of priorities.

Another area of Presidential interest was the racial discrimination which had existed for years in American schools. When Richard Nixon became President, very few Negro children in the South were attending schools with white students. Only about six out of every hundred black school children were in integrated schools. Within two years, this number had increased to about eighty out of every hundred children. In addition, loans to members of minority groups to help them go into business for themselves grew from less than eighty million dollars in 1967 to over one hundred and thirty million dollars by 1970.

In order to protect the country from further destruction of the environment through waste and pollution, the Nixon administration began strong programs to save the land, clean up the litter, and purify the waters of the nation. One month after Richard Nixon took office, the Justice Department sued a business firm for polluting the air. This was the first such action the Federal government had ever taken. The President urged the people of other countries to work with the United States to preserve the earth. Pollution, he observed, was not limited only to highly developed countries such as the United States. He suggested that the countries allied to the United States in NATO work together to clean up the rivers of Europe as well as the ocean filth around the globe. In 1972, he signed an agreement with the government of Canada to begin a vast clean-up of the Great Lakes in hopes of bringing them back to their earlier condition as excellent sources of fresh water.

The Nixon administration pressed on with the space program, only slowing it a bit in order to apply more money to care for direct human needs. In July, 1969, the dream which previous Presidents such as John F. Kennedy had worked to achieve was realized when the first American astronauts landed on the moon. Neil A. Armstrong became the first man to set foot on the lunar surface, making July 20, 1969, one of the most important days in world history. President Nixon talked to Neil Armstrong and his co-pilot, Edwin E. Aldrin, by radio-phone to the moon, remarking that it was about the most expensive call ever made. Armstrong, Aldrin, and the third member of the crew, Michael Collins, who stayed aloft in the main vehicle of their two-part craft, left a plaque on the moon signed by themselves and President Nixon. The inscription read: "Here men from the planet Earth first set foot upon the moon July, 1969, A.D. We came in peace for all mankind."

Richard Nixon believes strongly in the last sentence of that message and, during his time in office, tried to lay the groundwork for what he hoped might be a "generation of peace." To prove that he meant what he said, he ordered his representatives to meet with communist delegates to seek satisfactory means of reducing armaments. Long deliberation led to a treaty with Russia in 1971, prohibiting the placing of nuclear weapons on the ocean floor for testing or storage. On his own initiative, President Nixon renounced the use of germ warfare forever and ordered all United States supplies of germ weapons destroyed.

Closely linked with his pursuit of peace was a program in foreign policy which is now called the "Nixon Doctrine." This concept, announced in 1969, was designed to cool off the rivalries among the great powers by showing that the United States did not intend to get drawn into "little" wars such as the Vietnam war if it could possibly be avoided. This did not mean that the country was going to desert its allies. What the Nixon Doctrine meant was that if an American ally was threatened by an aggressive enemy, that ally could not expect American troops to take over all the fighting. The United States would send supplies and give as much assistance as was needed, but the country under attack would have to use its own young men to defend it.

The President began to apply the Nixon Doctrine to South Vietnam by a policy called "Vietnamization" of the war. American troops were gradually pulled out of South Vietnam over a four-year period. When Richard Nixon took office in January, 1969, there were 549,000 American servicemen in South Vietnam. Three and a half years later, the number had dropped to 39,000.

To bring the war to a close, American and South Vietnamese delegates met with North Vietnamese and Viet Cong (communists from South Vietnam) representatives at peace talks in Paris, France, on many occasions. The communists were definite in their demands for the communization of South Vietnam, while the Americans backed the South Vietnamese who were just as eager to keep the southern nation independent. The war was a thorny problem to Richard Nixon, causing great divisions at home and among the friends and foes of the United States abroad.

The President was criticized from every side. Many persons said that he had failed in his plan to unite the nation and, as the young girl's sign had read, "Bring us together again." To some people, he was not doing enough to end the war in Vietnam or to improve the economic life of the nation or to bring about reforms in American society. To others, he was doing far too much; they would prefer a less active President. But to most Americans, Richard Nixon was doing his best in what is the most difficult job in the world.

He was greatly aided, of course, by his wife. Wherever she accompanied her husband, she won friends, and most people considered the First Lady a great success. From the time that she reached her new address at 1600 Pennsylvania Avenue in January, 1969, Pat Nixon devoted herself to her task of managing the White House, serving as hostess for visiting dignitaries, and helping her husband in any way she could. One of her special projects was to encourage people to do more volunteer work to aid those less fortunate than they. College students and young people everywhere enlisted in a labor of love—to teach reading to the illiterate, to train the physically handicapped, and to care for children while their mothers were at work.

Pat Nixon's life was gladdened, but a little saddened as well, by the marriage of her older daughter to a New York law student named Edward Cox. The marriage of Tricia Nixon in June of 1971 was one of the year's most important social events. The ceremonies, both in the Rose Garden and inside the White House, were telecast and attracted tens of millions of viewers across the land and throughout the world.

With no more children at home, Pat Nixon's life was even closer to that of her husband of thirty years than it had been before. She traveled widely on missions for the nation, alone as well as with Dick Nixon. When an earthquake struck Peru in 1970, she flew there with food and supplies and most of all with the good wishes of the American people. Again, in 1972, she represented the United States officially for the first time in visits to several African nations. On her African journey, the First Lady attended the inauguration of President William Tolbert, of Liberia, the country founded by freed slaves from the United States in the nineteenth century. Pat also visited Ghana and the Ivory Coast on the same trip.

No event of her career could compare, however, with the

trip she undertook with the President to mainland China.

In July, 1971, Richard Nixon surprised the people of the United States and the world by a brief televised announcement that he had accepted an invitation to visit communist China, which, for many years, had been one of America's most determined enemies. Months of planning went into every last detail of the trip, the President and Mrs. Nixon even learning to eat with chopsticks quite skillfully.

For a week in late February, 1972, the world watched as Richard and Pat Nixon toured China, dined with Chinese leaders, attended the theater, and acted as sightseers. So strange and remote did China seem after decades of being closed to most Western people, that the Nixon visit was almost like the recent space voyages to the moon by American astronauts.

The real importance of the visit was the opportunity it gave the President to demonstrate the willingness of the United States to seek peace in every corner of the world, even with nations which have been considered hostile. No great agreements were made between China and the United States during the February visit but a foundation was laid for improving relations between the two countries. "We seek an open world . . . ," President Nixon had said in his Inaugural Address, "a world in which no people, great or small, will live in angry isolation. We cannot expect to make everyone our friend, but we can try to make no one our enemy."

In May of 1972, President and Mrs. Nixon undertook still another journey for peace, this time to the Soviet Union. Unlike the China trip, which only opened the prospect for future discussions, the Moscow visit was the occasion of the signing of a number of substantial accords, painstakingly worked out over many months by the Russian and American governments. The most important pledge made was the agreement by both sides to limit the number of strategic nuclear weapons in their arsenals. This was the first time since the beginning of the atomic age in 1945 that any progress had been made in arms limitation.

In addition, Russia and the United States agreed to a joint venture in space, set up rules for avoiding accidents and incidents involving their naval forces, laid the basis for cooperation in research on heart disease and cancer, and began talking about closer trade relations.

The President's trip was a busy one, mixing cultural activities and sight-seeing with long talks with the leaders of the Soviet Union. One of the unprecedented aspects of this unprecedented trip was the speech which Richard Nixon made directly to the Russian people over Soviet TV. Drawing on his lifetime of experience in public speaking, he sought to convince his audience that Russia had nothing to fear from the United States. He revived the memory of the cooperation between the two peoples in defeating Hitler's Germany in World War II, concluding with an incident which had deeply impressed him. While visiting a national monument in Leningrad, he had read part of the diary of a twelve-year-old Russian school girl named Tanya, who lost her family in the Nazi attack on Leningrad and who herself died later during the war. In his TV speech, he said he hoped that "no other children will have to endure what Tanya did. . . ."

Richard Nixon's willingness to travel as many extra miles as were necessary for the cause of peace meant that the motto left on the moon by the first spacemen to reach its surface applied also to him on earth—he "came in peace for all mankind."

BOOKS ABOUT RICHARD NIXON

ALSOP, STEWART. *Nixon and Rockefeller.* Garden City: Doubleday & Company, Inc., 1960.

CHESTER, LEWIS, ET AL. *An American Melodrama.* New York: Dell, 1969.

DETOLEDANO, RALPH. *One Man Alone.* New York: Funk & Wagnalls, 1969.

DRURY, ALLEN. *Courage and Hesitation.* Garden City: Doubleday & Company, Inc., 1971.

FABER, HAROLD, ED. *The New York Times Election Handbook 1968.* New York: New American Library, 1968.

HOYT, EDWIN P. *The Nixons.* New York: Random House, 1972.

KEOGH, JAMES. *This Is Nixon.* New York: G. P. Putnam's Sons, 1956.

KORNITZER, BELA. *The Real Nixon.* Chicago: Rand, McNally & Co., 1960.

MCGINNISS, JOE. *The Selling of the President 1968.* New York: Pocket Books, 1970.

MAILER, NORMAN. *Miami and the Siege of Chicago.* New York: New American Library, 1968.

MAZLISH, BRUCE. *In Search of Nixon.* New York: Basic Books, Inc., 1972.

MAZO, EARL, AND STEPHEN HESS. *Nixon, a Political Portrait.* New York: Popular Library, 1968.

MORIN, RELMAN. *The Associated Press Story of Election 1968.* New York: Pocket Books, 1969.

NIXON, RICHARD M. *Six Crises.* New York: Pocket Books, 1962.

SEVAREID, ERIC, ED. *Candidates 1960.* New York: Basic Books, Inc., 1959.

WHITE, THEODORE H. *The Making of the President 1960.* New York: Pocket Books, 1961.

WHITE, THEODORE H. *The Making of the President 1968.* New York: Pocket Books, 1969.

WILLS, GARRY. *Nixon Agonistes.* New York: New American Library, 1970.

WILSON, RICHARD, ED. *The President's Trip to China.* New York: Bantam Books, 1972.

INDEX

❦